P LAIN AND SIMPLE, THIS BOOK IS ABOUT THE Underground Railroad, one of America's most successful and powerful networks. The UGRR was so forceful it changed the course of history. Slavery was a serious problem in dire need of an immediate solution. That's when a passionate group of disconnected people connected and stood on the principle of freedom. Their collective and pioneering efforts formed one of the most amazingly dynamic networks in U.S. history.

Innovate: Lessons from the Underground Railroad dares to compare the Internet and the UGRR as two of America's most innovative, effective, and disruptive networks. Think about it: both serve as platforms for freedom, justice, and equality. From portals and links to branding and ownership, the comparisons are too obvious to ignore.

Innovate is full of insights, strategy, and at times playful ways to analyze creativity and purposeful disruption. It's a perspective-changing history lesson and a call to action. You've even been exposed to Dr. Syb's Seven Elements of Innovation in this brief description. It's a framework for assessment, analysis, and more. Innovation is faith in action. Turn the page and enjoy the ride.

INNOVATE:

Lessons from the
Underground Railroad

Andrea,

Everyone needs someone.
Stay connected by faith.

Dr. Syb

Innovate
Lessons from the
Underground Railroad

SYBRIL BENNETT, PH.D.

Library of Congress Control Number: 2012955174

Bennett, Sybril,
Innovate: Lessons from the Underground Railroad
ISBN-13: 978-09818074-5-4

Publisher: Buttons Brown Productions, Nashville Tennessee

Dr. Syb is a passionate speaker with an engaging message sharing insights about this book, how to use social and digital media tools, and what parents must know about cyberspace are among her most popular topics. See her TEDxNashville 2013 presentation on YouTube or hear her podcast at etpcast.com.

To book Dr. Syb or to contact the publisher, email: drsyb7@gmail.com.

Civil war
1861 - 1863

Cover and jacket design, inside text, and graphic by Tom Ventress, Ventress Design Works

The Emancipation Proclamation

January 1, 1863

By the President of the United States of America:

A PROCLAMATION.

Whereas, on the twenty-second day of September, in the year of our Lord one thousand eight hundred and sixty-two, a proclamation was issued by the President of the United States, containing, among other things, the following, to wit:

"That on the first day of January, in the year of our Lord one thousand eight hundred and sixty-three, all persons held as slaves within any State or designated part of a State, the people whereof shall then be in rebellion against the United States, shall be then, thenceforward, and forever free; and the Executive Government of the United States, including the military and naval authority thereof, will recognize and maintain the freedom of such persons, and will do no act or acts to repress such persons, or any of them, in any efforts they may make for their actual freedom.

"That the Executive will, on the first day of January aforesaid, by proclamation, designate the States and parts of States, if any, in which the people thereof, respectively, shall then be in rebellion against the United States; and the fact that any State, or the people thereof, shall on that day be, in good faith, represented in the Congress of the United States by members chosen thereto at elections wherein a majority of the qualified voters of such State shall have participated, shall, in the absence of strong countervailing testimony, be deemed conclusive evidence that such State, and the people thereof, are not then in rebellion against the United States."

Now, therefore I, Abraham Lincoln, President of the United States, by virtue of the power in me vested as Commander-in-Chief, of the Army and Navy of the United States in time of actual armed rebellion against the authority and government of the United States, and as a fit and necessary war measure for suppressing said rebellion, do, on this first day of January, in the year of our Lord one thousand eight hundred and sixty-three, and in accordance with my purpose so to do publicly proclaimed for the full period of one hundred days, from the day first above mentioned, order and designate as the States and parts of States wherein the people thereof respectively, are this day in rebellion against the United States, the following, to wit:

Arkansas, Texas, Louisiana, (except the Parishes of St. Bernard, Plaquemines, Jefferson, St. John, St. Charles, St. James Ascension, Assumption, Terrebonne, Lafourche, St. Mary, St. Martin, and Orleans, including the City of New Orleans) Mississippi, Alabama, Florida, Georgia, South Carolina, North Carolina, and Virginia, (except the forty-eight counties designated as West Virginia, and also the counties of Berkley, Accomac, Northampton, Elizabeth City, York, Princess Ann, and Norfolk, including the cities of Norfolk and Portsmouth[)], and which excepted parts, are for the present, left precisely as if this proclamation were not issued.

And by virtue of the power, and for the purpose aforesaid, I do order and declare that all persons held as slaves within said designated States, and parts of States, are, and henceforward shall be free; and that the Executive government of the United States, including the military and naval authorities thereof, will recognize and maintain the freedom of said persons.

And I hereby enjoin upon the people so declared to be free to abstain from all violence, unless in necessary self-defence; and I recommend to them that, in all cases when allowed, they labor faithfully for reasonable wages.

And I further declare and make known, that such persons of suitable condition, will be received into the armed service of the United States to garrison forts, positions, stations, and other places, and to man vessels of all sorts in said service.

And upon this act, sincerely believed to be an act of justice, warranted by the Constitution, upon military necessity, I invoke the considerate judgment of mankind, and the gracious favor of Almighty God.

In witness whereof, I have hereunto set my hand and caused the seal of the United States to be affixed.

Done at the City of Washington, this first day of January, in the year of our Lord one thousand eight hundred and sixty three, and of the Independence of the United States of America the eighty-seventh.

By the President: Abraham Lincoln
William H. Seward, Secretary of State.

DEDICATION

To my mother, my brother, and my Monica.
We did it!

In memory of my Daddy, Lloyd W. Brown

TABLE OF CONTENTS

The Underground Railroad is among the most effective, disruptive, and innovative networks in American history. Now prove it.

Test your historical knowledge about the institution of slavery. What was the government's role in sustaining the slave enterprise? Are remnants of the slave system still present in modern times?

The Underground Railroad really did exist. Find out how it was formed and sustained. Consider how it connects to the most dynamic network in American history: the Internet.

A conceptual framework is offered to analyze innovation. It's a seven-step approach to better understand how to conceive and implement new ideas. Here it is applied to the Underground Railroad and to the Internet.

There was no shortage of problems in dire need of innovation on the Underground Railroad. From physical bondage to the lack of citizenship, enslaved Africans were forced to think "out of the box." Discover some of the solutions the enslaved and UGRR supporters created.

Having a foundational principle to guide innovation is extremely useful. It provides internal motivation when all ways to success seem blocked. The principle of freedom was leveraged to encourage the enslaved to risk their lives to flee slavery.

Purpose pertains to direction. Where are you heading? The Underground Railroad was created to move the enslaved forward to secure their freedom. How did a disconnected group of people come together to fulfill their purpose? Without measurements, how did they identify success? What role does networking play in realizing one's purpose now and then?

Analyzing the mindset, strategy, and outlook of abolitionists, military officers, and the enslaved provides invaluable intelligence for the leadership community. Hindsight clearly shows why the Union won the war, providing many beneficial lessons for leaders.

Creativity was at an all time high on the Underground Railroad. There were many instances of just-in-time learning as the fugitives and agents formed new routes to freedom. What were some of the original, unique, and unbelievable ways fugitives escaped? How is the same pioneering spirit alive on the Internet?

It's contagious and uncontainable: passion cannot be denied. Innovators are passionate agents of change. Passion sustains networks, from the UGRR to the Internet; find out how internal drive can force victory.

Innovating can be fun, even in situations of life and death. Gaming involves goals, rules, feedback, and voluntary participation. It also calls for strategy and deception. All of these dynamics were at play on the Underground Railroad and are manifesting online today.

Change happens. Decisions are made by fate or by choice; history confirms this, while reality repeats it.

ACKNOWLEDGEMENTS

A special thanks to Mr. Carl Westmoreland, curator and senior adviser to the National Underground Railroad Freedom Center in Cincinnati, Ohio, UGRR historian and friend for your encouragement, time and wisdom. I will not forget your kindness. And I must thank Ripley, Ohio's Union Township Public Library Director, Alison Gibson. Alison, you are an expert in your craft and your time, tours and guidance were beyond appreciated. Thanks for introducing me to John Parker and so many other UGRR enthusiasts. I am so grateful to Kristin Kitchen, Owner of the Six Acres Bed and Breakfast in Cincinnati, Ohio. She showed great hospitality and sisterhood while I stayed at her amazing establishment. It was also a stop on the Underground Railroad. I am still in awe at the room in the attic where the enslaved hid. Thanks for letting me stand in the prayer circle and for your support throughout this journey.

This process took at least five years, and some were tortured with reading more versions than others. Thank you Shelley Jeffcoat, author of *When Fathers Were Gods and Children Ruled*, for always being ready to read and provide timely reality checks. A very special thanks to Matt Mason, author of *The Pirate's Dilemma*, for writing such a pivotal book and for taking the time to read mine in the early stages; it catapulted me forward. Thank you for your advice and for your time. Project manager, friend, and confidant, Monique Wilson, there really aren't enough words to express my appreciation to you for demanding results. Can't wait to see your blessings for always being a blessing.

Thanks to my friends and colleagues at Belmont University as a whole, and specifically History Professor Peter Kuryla for reading the manuscript and being blunt with me. I needed your honesty and it is a better book as a result. And I'm also grateful to Political Science Professor Nathan Griffith; thanks for helping me get the political parties straight. Is that an oxymoron? Erik Qualman, author of *Socialnomics* and *Digital Leader*, thank you for listening to me at such a crucial moment in time. You have no idea what your words and review meant to me. I questioned my premise, yet when I explained it to you, not only did you get it, you told me to go for it. Finally, Marcia Alesia Dawkins, author *Clearly Invisible: Racial Passing and the Color of Cultural Identity,* our friendship began divinely. Thanks for your enthusiasm, sharing resources, and running this race together. Your final edit of my work was exactly what I needed when I needed it most.

Thanks also to Kim Pearson, fellow member of the Association for the Study of African American Life and History and National Association of Black Journalists, for candid insight. Thanks to mentor and friend Al Tompkins for asking me from the beginning what the heck I was trying to do. At the time, my answer did not suffice; hopefully, the finished product answers the question. To my original partner in multimedia crime, Rick Hancock, thanks for helping me get to the point and say what needed to be said. To the multimedia mafia, John Girton, always grateful for all you contribute, from website design to wisdom. Retha Hill, "thanks" isn't enough for your timely conversations and pushes along the way.

To my Belmont University colleague, Dorren Robinson for editing an early version of the book, your candor and "WTH" expressions were priceless and a necessary part of this journey. Jill Ferguson, editor number two, helped move the project along. Eric Ventress is an amazing editor and researcher; thank you for your meticulous and thorough editing. Designer Tom Ventress, you've been putting up with my antics for more than a decade and I so appreciate you hanging with me this long. You are gifted and a very dear person.

To my ever-present mentor, play aunt, and friend, Alma Clayton-Pedersen, thank you for your unconditional love and support, as well as for applying the boot to the butt when needed. Author Yolanda Joe, I couldn't ask for a more supportive "big sister;" thank you for always standing in the gap. Thank you to my pastor, Robert E. Bell, and First Lady Rhonda Bell for organizing the trip to the Underground Railroad Freedom Center. Your spiritual leadership and vision are precious and priceless. And to the entire St. John Missionary Baptist Church family, thank you for your love and support. Thanks to the First Corinthian Missionary Baptist Church family for providing a solid spiritual foundation from the beginning.

To all of my friends, family and loved ones, I wish I could name everyone, but I can't. If I have omitted anyone, it was not intentional; know I acknowledge and appreciate each and every one of you. To our fierce, fiery and faithful family matriarch Mom, I haven't done anything in life without your love and support. I honor you with this work. To my brother Cy, the family military historian, thanks for listening at such a crucial moment and for explaining OODA to me. Knowing you are there means more than you'll ever know. To my daughter Monica, yes, Mommy put your name in print. I love you young lady. Hopefully, what I do will encourage you. Uncle Leslie, thanks for your encouragement. I finished in time. And finally, to the ancestors, may your memory be honored and your sacrifices and souls never forgotten.

In the voice of the little boy in the movie *The Sixth Sense*, "I See Opportunities." These are the words I use to begin most of my presentations. It's a positive way to encourage people to embrace the unknown. Faith really is the substance of things hoped for and the evidence of things not seen. It's the foundation for innovation. Fundamentally, that's what this book is about: finding the courage to not only create but to implement ideas. Creation is coming up with a plan, process, or project. Innovation means putting it into action. I've spent the past nine years really wrestling with the notion of innovation. What is it? What good examples exist? Why are some better innovators than others? These questions led me down an unlikely track... literally. I ended up on the Underground Railroad (UGRR). Yes, *the* Underground Railroad. After all, it's an inspiring tale of a community effort to achieve a common goal, culminating in a monumental victory. Still, how did I jump onto such a historical track? Well, my fascination with Black history and a habit for acknowledging the past for present accomplishments is part of the reason. Being called Harriet Tubman, trouble, trouble-shooter, a rebel and any number of other flattering terms played a role. And of course, fate is yet another reason I landed on the UGRR.

I am neither an historian nor an economist. I am a factual storyteller, an educator by birth and a journalist by fate. In my profession, I am charged with educating people to lead innovation in industries affecting our freedom. Journalism and education are both critical fields in any society. Innovation, especially due to digital developments, is changing both of these fields beyond virtual recognition. Reading extensively about innovation has revealed so many issues. There are those who will not change. There are those who want to and cannot. Then, there are those who embrace change and move on.

My reflective journey began long ago. In hindsight, my steps have clearly been ordered. On a summer trip with the St. John Missionary Baptist Church in Hendersonville, TN, we visited the Underground Railroad Freedom Center in Cincinnati, Ohio, which forced me to think more deeply about the contributions of enslaved Africans and their supporters. Some of the innovations used to lead fugitives to freedom were on display, and I was captivated by the ingenuity behind them. I sat on the floor taking notes, thinking how could a group of physically, mentally, and emotionally oppressed people accomplish so much? Why do people complain today when the conditions are not perfect, yet are so much better?

In 2007, while attending a Management Training Program at Harvard University, I went on the Boston African American National Historic Site tour. It introduced me to a lot of information that I just didn't know. I met abolitionist Lewis Hayden, a formidable foe in the fight for emancipation. I had heard of the newspaper publisher and UGRR activist William Lloyd Garrison, but I couldn't truthfully say much about him. I had no clue how important the contributions of some Bostonians were during slavery.

Later that same year, I participated in a women's Authenticity Retreat focusing on Leadership in Disruptive Times at the American Press Institute in Reston, Virginia. As part of the experience, we visited the Battlefield at Gettysburg. Again, I found myself immersed in a historical experience with my handy, dandy notebook. (I still use pen and paper more when taking notes in spite of all of my electronic gadgets.) After sitting down on the Battlefield at Gettysburg and feverishly taking notes, my destiny became clear: it was hidden in the past. The culmination of these timely encounters catapulted me into consciousness and forced me to read and interpret a lot of things through a historical lens.

As my reflection continued, I remembered the summer I spent teaching in London. We toured the home of Sir Walter Scott, who wrote the poem "Lady of the Lakes," from whose main character abolitionist and orator Frederick Douglass chose his last name. Before that, while attending the National Association of Black Journalists' (NABJ) annual convention held in Washington, D. C. in 2004, we went to the historic home of Frederick Douglass. Again, I was beyond intrigued. I wanted to know more about this powerful and amazing humanitarian. I wanted to channel his brilliance, bravery, and brand. It is especially needed now in an age sometimes marked with fear and excuses. At the NABJ 2011 annual conference in Philadelphia, Pennsylvania, I was taking a walk around the city, looked up and realized I was standing in front of abolitionist William Still's home. My destiny was in front of me.

After I read so many books about innovation, change, branding, the Internet, networks, disruption, tribes, linchpins, diversity, blinking, purple cows, tipping points, pirates, long tails, mavericks, outliers, the driven, gaming, and an array of other timely yet timeless concepts, it became clear a valuable part of the historic fabric was missing. Each term refers to a book I've read about innovation, change and leadership. They include: Seth Godin's *Linchpins, Purple Cow* and *Tribes,* Malcolm Gladwell's *The Tipping Point, Blink,* and *Outliers,*

Daniel Pink's *Drive*, Matt Mason's *The Pirate's Dilemma*, Chris Anderson's *The Long Tail,* and any book written by Clayton Christensen, just to name a few. When Seth Godin talked about linchpins, I thought about the conductors on the UGRR. Likewise, when Malcolm Gladwell described outliers, some enslaved Africans came to mind. The enslaved lived a faith-based experience.

Watching Alex Haley's documentary *Roots* as a child left a lasting impression and a longing to never forget the sacrifices made by the ancestors. This book is my effort to show the remarkable and miraculous stories of America's early innovators, the enslaved. They were assisted by an equally brave group of abolitionists, free and other enslaved Blacks, and so many others. Yet, it was the enslaved taking the first step toward freedom.

"Resolved, That the Slave System is a monopoly dangerous to the lives and liberties of the non-slaveholding people of the United States, and that therefore it is the duty of all the lovers of free institutions to resist its encroachments upon life and liberty, and to concentrate their powers for its entire abolition."

Brown County Anti-Slavery Meeting, Decatur Ohio
Thursday, December 25, 1851
reported in *The Ripley Bee,* January 10, 1852
(New Series, Vol. 3, No. 33)

CHAPTER ONE

The Underground Railroad Disrupts History

"It did not die, because it was essentially an idea, and ideas of that order are not subject to mortality. They never die. They merely withdraw until such time as they may be needed again. Then they come back."

WILLIAM BREYFOGLE

The Underground Railroad (UGRR) was among the most disruptive, effective, and innovative networks in United States history. This book is my effort to show the remarkable and miraculous stories of America's early innovators, the enslaved. They were assisted by an equally courageous group of abolitionists, free and enslaved Blacks, and many others. The word "enslaved" will be used with intentionality to accurately represent the experience of Africans in America. Enslaved means they were held in bondage against their will. Further, although small in number, there were other non-African slaves as well as indentured servants. Specifically, this book examines the experiences of those enslaved Africans who fought for their freedom, creating one of the most amazing networks in history. The UGRR is an inspiring tale of a community effort to achieve a common goal, culminating in a monumental victory. It was effective, disruptive, and innovative.

According to social scientist Everett Rogers, author of *Diffusion of Innovations*, an innovation is "an idea, practice or object that is perceived as new by an individual or other unit of adoption." The word "perceived" is noteworthy. While attending the Broadcast Education Association annual convention in Las Vegas, during a random conversation, I said, "It is what it is." Dr. Donald Page, a professor of mass communication at Tennessee State University in Nashville, Tennessee, countered, "It is what we perceive it to be." Using Rogers' definition, an innovation doesn't have to be new, people just have to think that it is; isn't that what marketing is?

Rogers outlines five categories describing different types of innovation adoption. They describe who is most likely to use something new. Which enslaved Africans were more than likely the first ones on the Underground Railroad? Rogers' first category is Innovators. They are adventurous people. Innovators are those who enjoy taking risks and trying new things first. They are comfortable with the unknown and uncertainty, and they have a willingness to accept failure. The innovator is a gatekeeper of sorts because others in the group may eventually follow his/her lead. Legendary UGRR conductor Harriet Tubman was an innovator. Innovators often operate in secret; they must avoid those who have a vested interest in maintaining the status quo, and avoid all who disdain or fear something new. For the record, Rogers says innovators typically befriend other innovators. Those who were close to Tubman took the same risks as she did, making significant contributions on the road to freedom.

Innovators are able to change. They are flexible, and those who are not innovators or innovative lack the ability and/or desire to adapt. Leaders often want a monetary return for trying something new; this isn't wise or practical in a virtual world. In *The Innovator's Dilemma*, Harvard University Professor Clayton Christensen argues the same. Established companies are less likely to change and more likely to compete than to create. Enslaved Africans who were less informed were less likely to leave. They may have known or have heard of the UGRR yet lacked the courage to "catch a ride."

2 The passion of innovators is contagious and tips into the next group of innovation adopters: early adopters. They keep their eyes on the innovators and act accordingly. Early adopters are more active and invested in the group than the innovators. These community members are crucial to the idea making it to other members of the group. The group members typically ask early adopters about new things and depend on their insight about the new idea or innovation. Some enslaved Africans waited to see if their friends and family made it to safety. Most didn't leave the plantation with the innovators. However, if the risk taker returned to get them, some of the enslaved left with them.

The early majority is the third category. The quote Rogers uses to describe this group is, "Be not the first by which the new is tried, nor the last to lay the old aside." This group is in the middle, firmly entrenched between the first and last categories. They are typically not leaders, but instead are sup-

3 porters. On the Underground Railroad, this would have been the "Amen corner." They didn't make the first or second escape run, but they got on the train just ahead of the next group. They followed their passionate leaders.

4 The fourth group is basically the followers. They are the late majority and to continue the Underground Railroad analogy, they probably were the last to leave the plantation. In modern times, peer pressure and economic reasons normally help move this group to action. This group must be convinced in order to feel safe. Most slaves in this category may not have left the plantation until the Civil War began in 1861. Some may have even tried to stay after they were declared legally free. This was a choice, thus they were slaves. Imagine what the conductors had to go through to get them to move. Anybody have relatives who still refuse to get a microwave, a cell phone, or a computer? What about friends who refuse to learn about social media, let alone use it?

5 Finally, the fifth category is made up of laggards. That's Rogers' term, not mine. These are the slaves who may never have left the plantation. Rogers says, "The point of reference for the laggard is the past." Need I say more? They are suspicious and resistant to change. In today's time, most are in the low-income bracket and literally cannot afford to take a chance. Many are isolated from the larger community, lacking passion and the spirit to innovate.

A special note about laggards in the digital age comes from an article for *Wired Magazine* by Clive Thompson. Thompson said laggards could become a lucrative group. They may purchase Google glasses, for example, and become an innovator or an early adopter, skipping many generations of technologies, as well as adoption categories. Some of the enslaved waited and may have taken an easier route to freedom since so many had already traveled the Underground Railroad. The tactics used by participants on the UGRR were innovative. Taken collectively, the efforts of the enslaved and their helpers were disruptive.

On his website, Clayton Christensen defines a disruptive innovation as "a process by which a product or service takes root initially in simple applications at the bottom of a market and then relentlessly moves 'up market', eventually displacing established competitors." The theory of disruptive innovation supports this research. It captures the essence of the development of the UGRR. A new audience has access and can afford to purchase the product. Typically, traditional companies are not aware of the product until it has disrupted the status quo. They are looking in the wrong direction, focused on their existing customers who can afford their existing product. On the UGRR, the slave owners represented the incumbents or traditional companies, and the enslaved were the entrants or new companies. The UGRR started in the shadows, providing access to a limited group of enslaved Africans. Slave owners could not fathom its existence.

In *The Innovator's Dilemma*, Christensen explains how traditional companies have difficulty meeting the needs of their current paying customers and those who may not have the resources to access the product. Many don't realize a serious disruption is on the horizon. Trying to get people to try something new can be very difficult. Yet reality has a way of forcing change. The slave owners felt their system was sound, that there was no way it could be toppled. Meanwhile, UGRR workers were able to reach a group of people who did not have access or the legal means to participate in the economy of the South. Thus, there was a dilemma. The slave owners could have recognized the enslaved Africans, empowering them to become consumers in the capitalist system; they chose not to do so. In this analogy, the UGRR is the entrant company reaching a previously unidentified audience to service.

In *Disrupting Class: How Disruptive Innovation Will Change the Way the*

World Learns, Christensen says, "A major lesson from our studies of innovation is that disruptive innovation does not take root through a direct attack on the existing system." The Underground Railroad had to take effect outside of the legal and established system of slavery. Direct attacks were futile, and asking the government for assistance had failed numerous times. The UGRR was an indirect attack with devastating accuracy. Initially, the slave owners weren't paying any attention to the UGRR network. Some may have dismissed it as incapable of having an impact on the institution of slavery. Today, some argue new businesses aren't "quality." True, some may not be at first, but left to grow and improve over time, some innovations disrupt the existing system.

The UGRR appealed to the innovators, a small group of mostly young men with the strength and stamina to escape. While the slave owner focused on running the plantation, they were too distracted to see the disruption. Historians like Ohio State University Professor Wilbur Siebert have been able to chronicle the effectiveness of the system. While Siebert could not quantify the number of those who escaped, he estimates it was in the thousands, a minority given the millions of enslaved Africans in America. A pebble in the form of the UGRR caused a revolutionary ripple in the stagnant waters of bondage.

Christensen defines established firms as those existing prior to a new technology. Entrant firms are those forming at the "point of technology change." The plantation was an established firm. Again, the UGRR was an entrant firm. Disruptive technologies typically change the fundamental ways business is done. When an enslaved person escaped, it changed the way the plantation operated; other enslaved persons had to work in the fugitive's place. Slave owners did not want to believe the enslaved were intelligent enough to escape.

To be clear, what Christensen discovered in his research was that established companies did not manage disruptive technologies well in reaching emerging markets, but entrant firms capitalized on the opportunity and the emerging market. The established companies had trouble servicing their core audience *and* the emerging market. The slave owners had trouble managing their enslaved enterprise and stopping escapes. Newer firms can see what established companies cannot; they don't have the same rules and regulations, and are able to focus on the emerging market and build their business model from the "bottom-up." This is the same organic method demonstrated by the UGRR. It was easier to enter from the bottom and move up (entrant firm) than to start upstream (established firm) and move downward in order to once again go upstream. And that's the innovator's dilemma.

Christensen suggests two courses of action to help implement new ideas within the corporate structure. One way is for managers to take unpopular stands and fight the system. The other way is to create an independent organization focused on emerging markets. Needless to say, he favors the latter. Ironically, the Underground Railroad accomplished both. The unofficial leaders took unpopular positions, operating independently to challenge, change, and disrupt the unjust system.

Many company leaders have their eyes on profits and not the periphery. They are often blindsided by new innovations. If and when they discover the new product or service, they want the same economic return. The UGRR was effective because it did not measure its success in real time; their focus was on freedom. It is vitally important that companies, and shareholders in particular, do not expect the same revenue to be generated by new technology, especially if the new innovation is being governed by rules made for and by traditional companies. Just because a new technology does not generate "projected" revenue does not mean the initiative is a failure; it may be ahead of its time. Fundamentally, this boils down to market expansion or market extinction.

Innovation needs a leader who is passionate about the purpose, not profit, prestige, or position. For these and many other reasons, Christensen strongly suggests spinning off the new idea from the core product. Create a budget line. Do not use past performance to assess the progress. Once the idea cements, it will tip the scale toward success. The UGRR didn't have record books. If the number of successful escapes was revealed, the UGRR could have been derailed; it was effective because it could not be detected.

With these thoughts about the UGRR's legacy of innovation and disruption in mind, this book provides a historical look at slavery and the innovations spawned to impede the "peculiar" institution. Then, by providing a historical background on the inception and implementation of the slave system leading to the creation of the UGRR, the case will be made that the Underground Railroad is among one of the most disruptive, effective, and innovative networks in American history. In doing so, this work contributes to the conversation surrounding innovation in America by excavating some of its earliest roots.

This new (or old, depending on how you look at it) contribution to today's conversation about innovation is critical. Much-needed wisdom can be found in the experiences of enslaved people in America. This wisdom may compel you to follow a virtual and physical path to find more information about the areas of interest to you right now. Understanding how, why, and when enslaved Americans innovated will encourage you. Knowing so many survived and succeeded against all odds should propel you forward, and possibly strengthen one's personal commitment to freedom. The UGRR was a network of people connecting to effect change. This is more relevant in the twenty-first century as a network of computers formally called the Internet raises the same issues of access, boundaries, and freedom.

Technology has changed the game… period. As digital tools evolve, so must attitudes toward innovation. Innovation is the implementation of a new, different, or remixed idea. Former Apple evangelist and best-selling author Guy Kawasaki defines innovation as creating products and services for people prior to them realizing they need them; this is how the late Apple founder Steve Jobs innovated. Innovation stems from creativity, and creativity is thinking outside of the structure formally known as a box. The box has disappeared.

It moved like the cheese Dr. Spencer Johnson wrote about in 1998. In *Who Moved My Cheese?*, Johnson introduced Hem and Haw as the fictional main characters. Haw tells himself, "Haw, haw, look at me. I keep doing the same things over and over again and wonder why things don't get better. If this wasn't so ridiculous, it would be even funnier." The cheese, the money, the opportunity have moved and many companies are still hemming and hawing about it.

In the twenty-first century, the refusal to change seems to be one of America's greatest challenges. An obsession with reliving the "glory" days of time past traps the nation in a familiar time warp facing in the wrong direction. Refusing to acknowledge and/or place the past in its proper perspective is another problem in dire need of a solution. Historically, it has taken disruptive force to spawn real change. Some people will make adjustments, but most will not accept or implement radical and/or necessary change. People who are averse to change are not called dinosaurs in a casual or a dismissive manner.

This book will engage, encourage, and empower you if you've heard or made any of the following statements:

- "It can't be done."
- "How are you going to do that?"
- "I can't see how that will work."
- "I'm afraid to try."
- "No one else has tried it, so why should we?"
- "We've always done it this way."
- "Past results confirm this is the best way."
- "What happened to the newspaper and music industries will not happen to us."

When I hear people say what "won't" happen and what "can't" happen, one of the most tragic periods in American history comes to mind: slavery. Some of the enslaved succeeded without the clothes on their backs, food on their tables, or knowledge in their minds. Often, popular culture reduces slavery to an inaccurate caricature, such as *Gone With the Wind* and *Amos 'n' Andy*. Depictions of happy, dumb, lazy and content slaves abound, while the enslaved's remarkable contributions are often distorted or simply ignored. It is much more fascinating to consider how the enslaved survived and adapted to a foreign land, language, culture, customs, and way of life without the freedom to enjoy life. This oversight is dangerous in any age, but especially in a digital one when information stored is public and permanent.

For example, Underground Railroad Freedom Center historian Carl Westmoreland cites the navigational genius of Robert Smalls as an example of just-in-time innovation. Smalls was a skilled seaman in Charleston, South Carolina. He dressed up like a captain and commandeered a Confederate ship, the *Planter*, taking it to Union territory. Arguments from

Smalls and abolitionist Frederick Douglass helped convince President Abraham Lincoln to allow African Americans to fight in the Union army. Smalls later became a captain in the U.S. Navy, a state legislator in South Carolina, and played an instrumental role creating the state's first public school system. This man was an enslaved African American. He did not have resources, yet he was resourceful. Can't you see how relevant and encouraging his story is now? It isn't chronicled in most American history books; neither are the stories of many who served on the UGRR. Yet his actions, like the UGRR, were effective, innovative, and disruptive.

The Internet is arguably the most effective, disruptive, and innovative network in the twentieth and twenty-first centuries. It is impossible to assess its impact with a snapshot. Much like Gutenberg's printing press, it may take centuries to understand the magnitude of its contributions. For the purpose of this book, the Internet is examined in a very tailored treatment for comparative analysis with the UGRR as a remarkable viral network and innovation.

Utter frustration in trying to reason with those who refuse to change forced me to look more deeply into history for creative solutions to contemporary problems. In other words, I got tired of fighting with the past in the present about the future. So, like any innovator, I began to look outside of the existing structure. The UGRR was created, operated, and utilized by enslaved African Americans. Although they did not have rights that the American government would recognize, they used the tools they had to innovate and to create paths to freedom that would be recognized and incorporated into the nation's history.

A framework was created to better identify, analyze, and assess innovation. It is being used in this book to provide a conceptual way to see how the UGRR was disruptive, effective, and innovative. This framework is called Dr. Syb's Seven Elements of Innovation. It is a way to examine innovation and to conduct various assessments, and it can be applied for grading, evaluation, inquiry, etc. This conceptual framework emerged after several discussions with journalism industry leaders. When told copying wasn't innovative, some argued they were ahead of the game by adopting practices already several years old. Because they were the first in their market to do so, they felt justified in their claim of being a leader. As I read more about innovation and innovative projects, it became clear there were some similar characteristics of successful innovations and playing catch up was not one of them.

Using observation, extensive reading, and acquired wisdom, the framework emerged. Dr. Syb's Seven Elements of Innovation are: problem, principle, purpose, perspective, pioneering, passion, and play. The UGRR solved a problem, based on principle with a clear purpose and perspective in passionate, pioneering, and at times seemingly playful ways. Innovation must have a purpose, creators full of passion, and a goal grounded in principle, not principal. True innovation solves a problem, and, furthermore, it involves risk; therefore, there is a pioneering component for being the first to create something new and/or different. In addition, innovation may involve the concept of play; it's fun to create without penalty or pressure, and for some gaming, seemingly insurmountable obstacles is a sport. Finally, the seventh area views innovation as a mindset, one's perspective. Of course, this list can be shortened, extended, eliminated, or ignored, but it still does not change its relevance and contribution to the discussion about innovation; it just provides a method for thinking about and examining the notion of innovation.

This discussion of the Underground Railroad will demonstrate how the system, the enslaved people, religious groups, and private citizens created and forged a path to freedom. The parallels between the Underground Railroad and the digital age will be explored with respect to innovation and networks. If the UGRR is among the most disruptive, innovative, and effective networks, the Internet is the most disruptive, innovative, and effective network in American history. Comparing the two came natural to me, given my areas of research. This is an ambitious and necessary comparison. This should not belittle the contribution of the enslaved and/or UGRR participants, but will cast them in a different light for a greater appreciation of, and respect for, their sacrifices. All involved in the UGRR deserve to be remembered.

The goal of this work is to make the parallels between the UGRR, the Internet, digital technology, and contemporary times so compelling that the connection can stand on its own. This is what James A. Dewar proposed to do in his analysis of the printing press and the Internet for the

Rand Corporation, a non-profit institution helping policy and decision-making through research and analysis. The examination of innovation, its adoption, and disruption play a critical role in this investigation. The examples, ideas, and insights converge to support the premise that the UGRR was among the most disruptive, effective, and innovative networks in U.S. history.

Chapter two provides a brief overview of the institution of slavery, while chapter three is a more in-depth history of the UGRR. Dr. Syb's Seven Elements of Innovation framework is given in chapter four. For each element, brief examples will demonstrate how each one relates to innovation via the UGRR and the Internet. Chapters five through eleven focus on each element respectively. The conclusion in chapter twelve evaluates the lessons learned and offers suggestions for future exploration, contemplation, and discussion.

Got your ticket? All aboard.

SUMMARY

- The Underground Railroad (UGRR) is among the most effective, disruptive, and innovative networks in American history.

- Enslaved means being held against one's will. A slave chooses to be shackled. Mindset is the key.

- An innovation is "an idea, practice, or object that is perceived as new by an individual or other unit of adoption." *Diffusion of Innovations,* Everett Rogers

- According to Rogers, the five categories of innovation adoption are: innovators, early adopters, early majority, late majority, and laggards.

- Disruptive innovation, as defined by Harvard University Professor Dr. Clayton Christensen, is "a process by which a product or service takes root initially in simple applications at the bottom of a market and then relentlessly moves 'up market', eventually displacing established competitors."

- The UGRR formed outside of the existing system of slavery.

- The most effective disruptions do not directly attack the existing system.

- Innovation demands passionate leaders valuing purpose and principle over principal.

- Dr. Syb's Seven Elements of Innovation provides a conceptual approach to further assess and evaluate innovation and more.

- The comparisons between the UGRR network and the Internet are too obvious to be ignored.

CHAPTER TWO

A Peculiar Institution

"I freed thousands of slaves. I could have freed thousands more,

if they had known they were slaves."

HARRIET TUBMAN

The slave trade in America traces its roots to the arrival of the first Africans in Jamestown, Virginia, in 1619. Originally brought as indentured servants, over time servitude became slavery outright. Eventually, Northerners focused primarily on new developments in industry and manufacturing, while Southern economies were centered largely around agricultural crops, such as tobacco and cotton, which required a constantly-enlarging work force to maintain its growth. When fugitives escaped from the cotton plantations and sought refuge in the North, some Northerners helped them; this created a serious division between slaveholders and those who aided fugitives. The terms "slaveholders" and "Southerners" may be used interchangeably for language variation, but it is important to understand that not all Southerners owned enslaved Africans. However, by the 1850s, the majority of the enslaved lived in or hailed from the South. The cotton economy was built by the free labor provided by the enslaved Africans. This is a point that South Carolina Senator (and later

Vice President of the United States) John Calhoun argued vehemently; he openly stated the economic health of the South could not exist without free Black labor. Confederacy Vice President Alexander Stephens believed slavery was the natural order for Africans in America.

The division between the North and the South on the issue of slavery was one of the many issues addressed during the Constitutional Convention in Philadelphia, 1787; how the people would be represented in the new government shaped by the creation of the United States Constitution was a critical issue. Whenever an enslaved person left a plantation, the absence represented significant financial loss for slave owners; not only did they lose the price of the slave, they lost the benefits and labor provided by the slave.

Slaveholders did not want to pay taxes on their "property" but wanted them to count in order to increase their political representation in Congress. To strike a compromise, Congressional leaders agreed to count the enslaved as three-fifths of a person, both for tax purposes and for the selection of members of the House of Representatives. It was also during this time Britain pressured U.S. lawmakers to end the international slave trade in 1808; this made the enslaved Africans already in America more valuable. By 1809, the slave trade in America created new wealth for slave owners and slave traders, and was a new source of free labor for the territory America acquired through the Louisiana Purchase in 1803.

It is important to note the Northwest Ordinance of 1787 took effect the same year, and was ratified into the Constitution in 1789. It banned slavery in the Northwest Territories, including Ohio, Illinois, Indiana, Michigan, Wisconsin, and part of Minnesota, but the prohibition did not free Africans already enslaved in the territory. During the same time, Pennsylvania adopted the Gradual Abolition of Slavery Act in 1780. This legislation made the future children of slaves free, ended the importation of enslaved Africans, and required owners to register slaves.

Those who were already enslaved in Pennsylvania were not freed until the mid 1800s, finally ending legalized bondage in the state. States including Connecticut, New Hampshire, and New York also engaged in the gradual abolition of slavery. New York already had an anti-slavery society called the New York Manumission Society, founded in 1785. Some members aided fugitives, and their work led to a gradual abolition act in 1799, and slavery was outlawed in the state of New York in 1827. In Massachusetts, slavery was ruled illegal based on the state's constitution and all the enslaved were freed in 1783. When Vermont entered the Union in 1791, it did so as a free state.

While these developments encouraged enslaved Africans to escape to the North; slaveholders petitioned Congress to do something about runaway slaves seeking refuge in the free territories. With increased pressure from Southern slaveholders, lawmakers created The Fugitive Slave Act of 1793. The Act allowed slave owners to legally reclaim their lost property, and suddenly any African (free or otherwise) could be detained and arrested; a state, local, county, or city authority could rule on the case and levy a $500 fine against those aiding a runaway slave. The Act was ultimately a response to the growing number of anti-slavery societies, abolitionists, and the formation of the Underground Railroad.

The Underground Railroad was named because of the terms people used to communicate, as well as for its invisibility. The Underground Railroad's official inception is a mystery; it had already been in existence before the Fugitive Slave Act in 1793. UGRR terminology came from railroads: for example, escapees were passengers, safe places were depots, and someone that led passengers from one depot to another was a conductor. A more in-depth history on the UGRR is provided in chapter three. For now, let's jump to exploring the similarities between the plantation and factory systems with the digital age.

The plantation model was a system of exploitation in which human capital was expended for financial gain, and the inability of some plantation owners to embrace change proved to be detrimental. An example would be some slave owners planting cotton when the ground wasn't ready; they ignored nature, going against seasons and the natural order and ruining their land in the process. When a certain field would no longer yield the desired crops, owners moved on to the next plot instead of repairing the damaged land. They exploited the land and killed diversity, compromising the long-term sustainability of the entire economic system for short-term profits.

As the industrial age ends, many companies refuse to embrace the digital age. Like the Southern slave owners, some executives continue to use outdated philosophies to manage modern-day work experiences. For example, some employers punish employees for using social media tools, despite research that they can increase productivity and company visibility. Having fun makes some people work harder; that's part of the reason why Google employees have one day a week to focus on side projects. Remember, disruption happens outside of the existing system. Google can benefit from what the workers create; it's an exercise in contained disruption.

Another unfortunate similarity between the plantation model and the twenty-first century management system is the need for some "overseers" to control employees. Employees with creative ideas to improve workplace practices were often ostracized, ignored, or had ideas stolen; similar (though obviously harsher) treatment was given to the enslaved. See the contemporary connections? Blocking creativity, compromise, and common sense circumvented the system. Some slave owners accumulated great wealth in the short-term but paid dearly long-term. They accomplished this through brute force, abusing slave labor.

The enslaved were not fairly compensated for their work. They were beaten if they didn't perform; if they received a "reward," it may have been in the form of food or clothing they needed to survive. Beyond survival, there was no internal incentive to work besides trying to raise enough money to purchase freedom. The remnants of this system and mindset are present in the modern day workplace. Many work environments have supervisors who may or may not care about the well being of the workers; they are more concerned with profits than people. Tragically, the more things change, the more they stay the same.

It is critical to understand the mistakes of the past in order to avoid repeating them. People work harder when they are motivated by a personal connection to the work to be completed. In the book *Drive*, Daniel Pink discusses the need for a different type of motivation. In the past, Motivation 1.0 was based on survival; this describes the experience of enslaved Africans. Motivation 2.0 was based on rewards and punishment; the institution of slavery operated with a far greater emphasis placed on punishment than rewards.

Pink argues Motivation 3.0 should focus on autonomy, mastery, and purpose; the individual operates independently to master a skill driven by an internal purpose. During slavery, Motivations 1.0 and 2.0 were in full effect; to use Pink's analogy, the masters, overseers, supervisors, managers, and others in authority received the carrots while the slaves, workers, and servants got the stick. The plantation model evolved into the factory model. As more and more companies move their businesses overseas, the factory model is being replaced in the Information Age. Economist Jeremy Rifkin predicts as little as five percent of the adult population will be needed to manage and operate the traditional industrial sphere by the year 2050. In other words, factory jobs may be eliminated within the next forty years.

People need to be responsible and accountable for their destiny. America needs more innovators and entrepreneurs, not only to create new products but also to create more jobs. The old system of power and control motivated by fear must be destroyed. Educational institutions must prepare a workforce for the future, not for the past. To better understand the need for change, analyzing the system of slavery is beneficial. This is especially relevant in the Internet age.

Structurally, the Internet and the Underground Railroad share many similarities. The Internet is comprised of connected computers (most commonly accessed thru the World Wide Web, a collection of links to pages of various content), while the UGGR was made up of hundreds of connected locations to make a greater whole. Both networks were decentralized; no one individual controlled the network. The Internet allows any number of people to leverage the system for a common goal. This is similar to what the UGRR accomplished: it was a system appearing outside of the system of slavery, connecting people to solve an unthinkable problem.

According to James Surowiecki in the book *The Wisdom of Crowds*, decentralization is one of the main elements of leveraging collective wisdom: it allows for groups to work independently while producing collective results. In addition to decentralization, the other conditions for wise crowds are independence, diversity, and aggregation. Members need to come to their own conclusion without being influenced by others. They have to exercise independent thinking. They don't go along with the group to be liked, accepted, or respected; independent decisions are based primarily on the information provided, instinct, and experience.

Diversity involves people with different experiences and beliefs working together to identify different solutions. Diversity and independent thought are critical factors to help people avoid groupthink, the tendency to go along with a group just to get along with the group. Aggregation involves combining the information from the decentralized, diverse, and independent group to make a more informed decision. The UGRR is a prime example of leveraging diversity, decentralization, independent thought, and aggregation to harness the wisdom of a crowd, and the Internet is too.

As mentioned at the end of chapter one, James A. Dewar compared the printing press to the Internet. In doing so, he said decentralization is what makes the Internet what it is. He said we should not be too quick to structure the system before we know what it is and what it can accomplish; this point illustrates the importance of freedom in the virtual world. The webbed system is analogous to the Underground Railroad, as well as to the plantation system the UGRR was formed to circumvent. The Internet resembles the institutionalized system of ownership practiced during slavery; no one owns the entire system, and its magnitude is impossible to assess in real time. It is a platform for unprecedented capitalism.

Capitalism is the cornerstone of American commerce. The system primarily depends on control, the labor force, and the market. Control during slavery translated into ownership. However, not many people owned enslaved Africans; it was only a vocal minority of Southern citizens that were slaveowners. Yet the power wielded by the few greatly influenced the direction for the whole. Owning property, in the form of slaves and land, secured the slave owners' prosperity. In *Let My People Go*, Henrietta Buckmaster put this into perspective: "With more than four million slaves, whose average individual value was $500 (but could be as high as $2000), it is evident that the minority which controlled them controlled the country." Jumping on a different yet relevant track for a moment, let's think about the notion of ownership and its impact in the twenty-first century.

In the digital age, owning physical property, such as buildings and equipment, is costly. Owners have to pay for maintenance, staff, supplies, and more. Yet the notion of owning digital property can be equally as vexing; this idea will be explored more in chapter five. Physical ownership is seemingly an unnecessary expense in an age of mobility, flexibility, and adaptability. With companies like Google and Apple innovating in nanoseconds, it will be interesting to see which traditional companies survive. Arguably, the ones who relinquish control to consumers, while also providing the platform and resources for consumers to produce, will continue to win. In addition those who leverage the value of physical ownership will come out ahead as well. Understanding property, land, labor, and value were just as critical during slavery as they are in modern times.

Making these historical connections and applying lessons learned is not an option. Re-evaluating and possibly replacing the system of ownership is necessary. Harvard University Professor Yochai Benkler believes the next system should be a networked information economy, and the attributes of the network Benkler mentions in his book, *The Wealth of Networks,* sound very familiar. "What characterizes the network information economy is that decentralized individual action—specifically, new and important cooperative and coordinate action carried out through radically distributed, nonmarket mechanisms that do not depend on proprietary strategies—plays a much greater role than it did, or could have, in the industrial information economy." This is the definition of disruption in another form. These characteristics are exactly what made the UGRR effective, innovative, and disruptive. What Benkler proposes is an open network.

In his analysis of networks, Benkler looks at the same issues faced on the UGRR: freedom, boundaries, and access. While reading his book, I found similarities to the slave system in the introduction. Part of his reason for writing the book was to challenge the system, the status quo, "the man" to deal with the problem of freedom and access before it becomes insurmountable. He argues more universal access to technology is forcing people to once again deal with the issue of freedom. In a new economy, one based on digital goods where the people formerly known as consumers can now make significant contributions as producers, the power has shifted. The Internet is an open platform. Therefore, those who are able to connect to the network can use it. However, there are those who want it deregulated, compromising net neutrality.

Net neutrality preserves the free and open Internet. It allows the government to regulate Internet Service Providers (ISPs) like AT&T, Comcast, and Verizon. With regulation, it's possible for more people to have access to create their digital destiny; it is fundamentally a control issue. In the United States, individuals and groups pay ISPs for Internet access. All people receive equal access to websites based on the access for which they pay; all sites download based on the purchased speed, and websites like Google and Facebook do not pay the ISPs in order for their sites to run faster. If net neutrality is compromised, corporations like Comcast and AT&T could create and dictate the price companies like Google and Facebook would have to pay in order for users to access their sites.

Media deregulation in the U.S. in the mid 1980s has led to oligopolies, a handful of companies dominating various media industries. Without government regulation, a few corporations now own the majority of the media in America. In the recording industry, Sony Music Entertainment, Universal Music Group and the only U.S.-based company Warner Music Group are the companies with centralized power and influence. In the book industry, six key players may become five as Random House and Penguin Books discuss a merger.

In radio, Clear Channel Communications is the majority owner with more than 800 stations; Bain Capital is its primary owner. Denied access forced some to create pirate radio stations outside of government regulations; this was the impetus for Matt Mason's book *The Pirate's Dilemma*. Like some pirates, innovators help create innovation where little (if any) exists due to corporate domination. If net neutrality is removed through deregulation, it's anyone's guess what systems will appear to counter the handful of companies controlling access to the Internet and its content.

Regarding net neutrality, corporations contend they are building the Internet infrastructure and providing the bandwidth but not being compensated fairly for their contributions. Deregulating the Internet by getting rid of net neutrality would cause the appearance of scarcity in spite of the abundance in cyberspace. Some argue big companies would be able to censor information by controlling access and speed to finding information, but corporations deny this accusation. In a networked system, this could provide the corporate owners with an imbalance of power, similar to the slave system run by the minority of slave owners.

In the South, the plantation owners wanted to dictate how the institution of slavery would exist in the North. Ironically, had the Southerners left the North alone, the historical record may have been significantly different; it's funny how some want their rights, but don't want others to have the same freedom of choice. Southerners with political and economic power didn't want anybody to control them, but wanted to control others. This is very similar to the debate over net neutrality and, of course, money is at the center of the debate.

The South continued to embrace the past while the North looked to the future. Northerners innovated to compete with the diversified international trade markets; the South, meanwhile, placed their bets on "king cotton" and traditional foreign trade. Benkler says, "An economic policy, allowing yesterday's winners to dictate the terms of tomorrow's economic competition, would be disastrous." This quote is self-explanatory. Stop using the past to project your future; value the lessons learned from the experience. Depending on data from the industrial age to operate successfully in the digital age is futile.

Revisiting *The Innovator's Dilemma*, established firms were not leading innovation. They were focused on competition, past market performance, and rewarding employees for maintaining the status quo rather than encouraging them to create disruptive innovations. The connection to the UGRR is so clear. Slave owners were facing the wrong direction to see the future.

The UGRR interrupted the system of slavery; the Internet has disrupted a lot of industries, including music, movies, and newspapers. Newspapers had all three legs of their dominant financial stool removed simultaneously; they could no longer depend on subscriptions, advertising, and classified ads as revenue streams, and executives were warned about the pending digital impact. Yet many were shocked when fewer people were subscribing to receive the hard copy of the paper. Advertising revenue, in turn, went down as a result of fewer eyeballs to read the paper. Craigslist, the online classified ads website, changed the game for classified ads, removing another key source of revenue for newspapers. Warnings are to be heeded. Unfortunately, the position of Monday-morning quarterback remains open as hindsight gives way to foresight.

This quote from *Linchpin: Are You Indispensable?* author Seth Godin is relevant:

> "The newspaper industry can't untangle news from paper, can't see the difference between delivering the news around the world for free and putting

it on a truck for shipment down the block. As long as each of these elements is seen as inseparable from the others, it's impossible to untangle the future. That's why outsiders and insurgents so often invent the next big thing—they don't start with the tangled past."

Godin touches on the reason some Southern politicians and slave owners could not move forward; they simply refused to do so. They wanted the slave empire to continue in its current state, ignoring the change they were experiencing and the change happening around them. Whether it was denial, denunciation, or doubt, a leader's choice is lasting. Those who are unable to live in the present compromise their future.

The Underground Railroad was formed as a direct response to this inability to embrace reality. Who really thought it was a good idea to enslave and enrage a group of people outnumbering whites in the South at a time when cotton crops profits were declining? Underestimating one's opponent causes problems; not being able to see the opponent can be catastrophic. Operating outside of the system of slavery, the UGRR was effective because it could not be detected. The enslaved understood their reality and some took the risk to change it.

The unofficial leaders on the UGRR were the conductors. The number of fugitives, free Blacks, abolitionists, and others serving as conductors is unknown. They could not leave a paper trail because people's lives depended on secrecy. Many enslaved Africans went through the UGRR and had no idea they were on one of the historic routes. Most conductors and agents operated independently yet collectively. Comparing the UGRR and the Internet (here, specifically the Web) isn't a stretch. Benkler says, "The independence of Web sites is what marks their major difference from more organized peer-production processes, where contributions are marked not by their independence but their interdependence. The Web as a whole requires no formal structure of cooperation." That's the UGRR in a nutshell: an organic, peer-to-peer network leveraged through cooperation, collaboration, and community.

Another way the UGRR is analogous to the Internet stems from the role of the conductors. Like conductors for the UGRR, search engines help users navigate the Web. Both decide where a user or passenger should go for the next link or "safe place." Conductors improvised and sent the fugitives on various paths depending on whether the fugitive was being pursued.

Interestingly, more than a hundred years later, this is how Google's search engine works. Different people can be directed to different links even when both are searching the same topic. The results are determined by previous searches; if you only search for entertainment or sports, your search results will be tailored accordingly. As a result, a large group of people may miss critical news and information. If this were the case during slavery, those escaping may have been led down the wrong path due to limited information. They would have only gone down "known" paths based on previous experience. That would have been potentially devastating for some.

Continuing to compare the parallels between the UGRR network and the Internet, search engine optimization (SEO) is critical because it is how you get the most people to visit your website. Major search engines like Google use algorithms to rank websites. In Peter Kent's *Search Engine Optimization for Dummies*, he offers six variables to improve traffic on a website: keywords, content, page optimization, submissions, links, and time. On the UGRR, the fugitives used keywords; on the Internet, passwords are used. When a hacker discovers a password, the system is compromised; when codes used by the UGRR participants were discovered, immediate adjustments were made to avoid detection.

In the world of SEO, content is key. On the UGRR, the enslaved were the content, passengers being shared with other people along the routes, similar to the content passed from person to person online. Page optimization deals with content placement on the website. When enslaved Africans were at the right place at the right time, they were more likely to make it to the next safe place. Information placed in the right place on the website is more easily seen by the search engine and improves the websites rank. Continuing the search engine analogy, another way to improve search engine optimization relates to the number of submissions on a Web page. Web pages benefit from the number of new articles, videos, information, and content uploaded. As the number of passengers increased, the efficiency and credibility of the UGRR network did also. Practice made certain conductors more efficient over time. This innovative look at the

UGRR and the Internet may be jolting for some, yet through a virtual lens, the comparisons are not only plausible, they're directly applicable.

This book is about innovation and disruption. It is about network effectiveness. It is about the Underground Railroad and how the system that helped enslaved Africans escape from captivity in the nineteenth century is not so different in creativity, out-of-the-box thinking, and structure as innovations like the Internet are today. Building the case to prove this book's premise, the UGRR was effective because it was undetected. The network was used to facilitate escapes for thousands of enslaved Africans. The UGRR was innovative for operating without an official leader, strategic without official plans, and effective without an organizational structure.

SUMMARY

- In the United States of America, slavery developed after the first Africans arrived in Jamestown, Virginia in 1619.

- Many of the pro-slavery laws adopted by Congress were created to address the South's particular needs, such as the Fugitive Slave Act.

- Several Northern states moved to abolish slavery in their territories. It never existed in the states formed from the Northwest Ordinance, which consisted of the modern-day Midwestern states.

- Remnants of the plantation system were adopted into the industrial age system. For example, overseers became managers, and the well-being of workers, both then and now, takes a back seat to profit.

- Author Daniel Pink argues for motivation 3.0 focusing on autonomy, mastery, and purpose, leaving the survival and reward and punishments represented by motivations 1.0 and 2.0 behind.

- Right-brained thinkers are more creative and prepared to do what computers cannot do. They are needed now more than ever.

- The Internet is a computer network facilitating human connections for freedom. The Underground Railroad was a human network for freedom.

- Diversity, independent thought, decentralization, and aggregation are critical factors increasing the wisdom of crowds.

- The network information economy involves decentralized action.

- Net neutrality ensures freedom on the Internet.

- The UGRR was a network leveraging cooperation, collaboration, and community, just like the Internet of today.

CHAPTER THREE

The History of the Underground Railroad

"History repeats itself because no one listens the first time."

ERIK QUALMAN

The Underground Railroad appeared and evolved to facilitate the escape of fugitive slaves. It was a just-in-time network appearing when an enslaved person was on the run and disappearing when slave catchers or slave owners were trying to reclaim their missing property. The UGRR is often reduced to a legend as if it did not exist. Given the wealth of research by Ohio State University Professor Dr. Wilbur Siebert and many others, it is impossible to ignore the empirical evidence supporting its existence. Further, in the twenty-first century, lessons from the nineteenth century are needed now more than ever as some politicians and private citizens fight for "states' rights," "their country," and other such initiatives potentially setting the stage for a modern-day Underground Railroad in America.

Historians believe a man named Isaac Hopper was among the first abolitionists to participate in the UGRR network. In 1787, Hopper was a

Quaker living in Pennsylvania and aiding fugitives he called "friends," embracing his religious roots by risking his life to help strangers. He was short in stature yet a giant in the freedom movement. Hopper had a keen understanding of the legal system, often forcing his adversaries to follow the letter of the law. If there was a loophole, he would take advantage of it; he could not stand to see anyone suffer an injustice.

Not forgetting Hopper's contribution, the story shared most often about the inception of the UGRR involved an enslaved man named Tice Davids. Davids escaped from his master in Kentucky via the Ohio River, possibly ending up in Ripley, Ohio around 1831. At that time, the Ohio River was not as deep or as wide. His master chased him and allegedly said, "He must have gone on an underground road."

The UGRR consisted of a network of people, places, and things to help fugitive slaves along their path to freedom. Indeed, the UGRR was a man-made network, depending on word-of-mouth communication to build relationships. Groups, including members of the society of Quakers, a religious group also called "friends," other Whites, and Blacks (slave and free) established the social network. Participants were not in a position to hold public or lengthy meetings to discuss their options, they didn't elect a President, Vice President, or any other officers. They had to seek their freedom without a formal structure in place, and regimenting innovation defeats the purpose.

Based on the characteristics of the UGRR network, its success defies logic. Its invisibility alone was amazing. Fast-forward more than a hundred years, noting that the Internet evolved in similar fashion, without ownership or formal organization. Its framework cannot be seen, yet everyone knows it is there. It is a platform, facilitating freedom movements globally.

The UGRR facilitated freedom without any formal, identifiable leadership, serving as a prime example of a "leaderless movement." Indeed, while there were conductors and agents, there wasn't one individual in charge of the UGRR's execution. No one called the shots or coordinated the efforts of the entire network, making the UGRR very effective. Without an official leader, slave owners and slave catchers could not comprehend the system; there wasn't a leader to attack, so they could not identify a target to end the movement. In addition, without a central leader, the

UGRR was not a control-based hierarchy; instead, it was an "adhocracy." In *Reframing Organizations*, authors Lee G. Bolman and Terrence E. Deal define this organizational structure as a "loose, flexible, self-renewing organic form tied together mostly by lateral coordination." Lateral coordination entails informal communication, flexibility, and coordinating roles without the command and control paradigm. This organizational structure allowed the trains to run autonomously.

Each UGRR train operated independently, yet the end goal was clear. A leaderless movement may involve an individual or a small group coordinating separately to accomplish an agreed upon goal; the people are empowered to make decisions. Since the UGRR had to operate outside of the view of the government and the police, this type of movement was ideal. Participants leveraged information in newspapers, in pamphlets, and in flyers to widely disseminate necessary facts. They were empowered to make on-the-spot decisions, an absolute necessity in life-or-death situations.

Without a central headquarters to destroy, it is difficult to infiltrate such movements. A twenty-first century example of a leaderless movement is Occupy Wall Street in America; the initial formation of the Tea Party is another example. The popularization of the leaderless movement concept is attributed to Louis Beam, Vietnam Veteran and Ku Klux Klansman, while Colonel Ulius Amoss is credited for developing the strategy in response to the threat of communism in America. Whoever created the concept, hundreds of years ago it was implemented on the Underground Railroad.

Identifying like-minded individuals who can effectively manage small groups to achieve a common goal is the basis for leaderless movements. Harriet Tubman was a conductor, but was not the only point person on the UGRR; she was a symbolic leader, which can be a common occurrence in leaderless movements. In Harriet Tubman, the slaves had a competent, courageous, and committed role model, one who lead not by being granted a title, but by innovating to find solutions. Contemporary leaders would be wise to study Tubman's legacy of leadership.

Harriet Tubman, originally named Araminta Harriet Ross, was born in 1822. She helped guide hundreds of the enslaved to freedom. Slaveholders offered tens of thousands of dollars for her capture. Tubman met like-minded people whom she could trust in order to realize her goal: freedom for her people. In a sense, she managed her brand, her reputation, and her desire for the enslaved to be free. She used her instinct and the tools placed in her path. The Black Moses, as she was called, didn't have technology in order to communicate. She was a disruptive force just like the Underground Railroad. She was an out-of-the-box innovator, Black, female, and an enslaved person implementing creative strategies for success.

Harriet Tubman's story isn't chronicled in most leadership books, guides, case studies, websites, or manuals. Tubman is definitely a Jim Collins' level five leader, as described in his book *Good to Great*. Collins' level five leader doesn't take credit for initiatives; they operate with integrity, encouraging and empowering the team to succeed as well as acknowledging their contributions. In Tubman's case, she gave the credit to God. She prayed, expected, and received deliverance. She clearly mastered what Collins calls the Stockdale Paradox: believing no matter the situation. Innovators have to believe in the impossible. By speaking directly to her passengers, Tubman embodied true leadership without electronic tools. Face-to-face communication is still the most effective way to convey a message. In her day, part of Tubman's brilliance was due to her mastery of the art of communication. Leaders must exercise the art of listening and sharing information.

Tubman was a woman in a male-dominated society, and she had every excuse to remain silent: she was African, female, and enslaved. Even for women in contemporary society, the problem of sex discrimination persists. An embarrassing example is the Augusta National Golf Club's refusal to allow female members. After an unsuccessful lobby by activist Martha Burk in 2002, the club finally admitted two women in 2012, after 80 years of gender-based exclusion. Pay inequity is one of the myriad other issues that still remain for women. The documentary *Miss Representation* captures the modern day experience of women, showcasing the need for innovators.

Innovators speak through action; they make it happen. They don't talk, they do. Like all slaves, Tubman was considered chattel. In spite of her invisible status, she shared her vision to solve the problem. She acknowledged it, she identified it, and then she innovated to solve it. She organized people without actually organizing them. She couldn't hold meetings or connect with people virtually; she did everything manually and personally.

The enslaved African encountered and transcended communication, physical, geographical, mental, and financial barriers in order to secure their freedom.

Instinct, intuition, and the internal voice are valuable characteristics for leaders. Tubman embraced her spirituality and utilized it on the UGRR. In order to innovate, one must have faith it can work; risk takers are fearless enough to follow a hunch. Tubman led from within and her followers believed in her intuition. The ability not only to hear, but also to heed the voice within, is immensely important; not only for the unofficial leaders on the UGRR, but also for innovators of the information superhighway. Apple co-founder Steve Jobs and Twitter co-founder Evan Williams both credit following hunches for part of their success. This is the case author Malcolm Gladwell makes in the book *Blink;* in certain instances, having too much data can be a hindrance.

Tubman used her voice as well as natural resources to bring people together in order to facilitate freedom. She did not have technology. Now, the Internet is a platform where people are able to communicate, organize, and implement change. This is exactly what took place through the Underground Railroad network. A group of disconnected people took unprecedented chances for a common goal without the luxury of modern day resources, technologies, or communication tools. As previously mentioned, social networks like Facebook, LinkedIn, and Twitter provide the digital foundations for electronic communication in the early twenty-first century. The Underground Railroad was a crucial network offering a way for people to organize for a cause and the Internet is, too. In the digital age, messages are sent instantly via mobile devices, text, and email. The enslaved did not have these technological luxuries.

Hearing terms like "social network" and "word of mouth" should at the least warrant a passing comparison, if not acknowledgment, of a possible connection between the past and the present. Similar terms and concepts are being used in the virtual world, and the UGRR was based upon social relationships, connections and communication. Developing social relationships is mission critical, then and now. The train analogy can be used to describe the speed of change facilitated by the Internet. Catching a ride on the virtual locomotive can be a challenge, yet it is an absolutely necessary trip. Surely some fugitives felt the same way as they ventured from the plantation into the unknown, searching for freedom aboard the virtual train. It was so effective because participants embraced humanity. They leveraged relationships with strangers and neighbors alike to achieve the end result. This is exactly what online tools allow people to do globally.

Twitter is a microblogging tool that provides a platform for 140-character messages to be broadcast to anyone with Internet access. Information shared through this platform is searchable, even without an account, and research can be conducted in real time. Tweets, as the short messages sent are called, are archived by the Library of Congress. Messages on the UGRR were so effective because they were not stored. Communication on the freedom network may have been sent to strangers or friends; this is the communication facilitated by Twitter. To learn more about Twitter basics, go to *learnitlive.com/drsyb*.

Twitter users can read, reply to, or favorite (saving it to a list of tweets that are most important to them) any other user's tweets. They can also resend (retweet) a post, allowing their own followers to see it. It is an ideal format for breaking news, sharing critical information with the masses like broadcast television, yet the messages are available on demand any time, anywhere through a mobile device. On the UGRR, breaking news was a matter of life and death, but the information could not be easily broadcast.

Sending a tweet on the UGRR would be the equivalent of sending a message to any conductor, agent, or UGRR participant. While Twitter is immediate, it would have taken a while for information to reach the larger network on the UGRR, as messages were carried on foot or via horseback. This is why UGRR supporters depended on proximity for most relationships: they needed to be close together for the network to function efficiently.

The Underground Railroad was a local system. It depended on small communities of self-coordinated people to help fugitives to make it to freedom. Recall, these are the ideal circumstances James Surowiecki describes to leverage the wisdom from a crowd. Surowiecki said better decisions are made by small, diverse groups of people thinking independently with a clear goal in mind. On the Internet, smaller, more familiar groups can be created on platforms like Facebook. Twitter is a one-to-many mode of communication, while Facebook can be far more limited, given the users' ability to

"friend" certain people. Facebook mirrors the more localized, connected relationships between UGRR agents and conductors.

The UGRR was an organic, grassroots effort. Like many of today's
online social movements, one person starts to do something and someone
else confirms the leader's platform or direction by following the leader.
Once the two members team up, others follow them to achieve a common
goal. This is the way most social networks evolve. The way some contemporary movements (such as grass-roots charity movements or political
campaigns) are formed and sustained mimics the design and nature of the
UGRR. Credibility on social networks is built when members share their
expertise, add value to end-users, receive acknowledgment or validation
for their efforts, and complete jobs posted online.

One way to measure social network "street cred" is by examining the
number of legitimate followers a person has across different social media
sites, including Twitter, Facebook, LinkedIn, and more. On the UGRR,
such data was impossible to compile, yet solid reputations could be built
on the number of successful escapes facilitated by certain conductors and
agents. Reputations were strengthened via word of mouth. This is how the
most famous conductor on the UGRR came into prominence.

The enslaved whispered messages to each other while generations
hundreds of years later spread tweets via Twitter to encourage change and
revolt in Tunisia, Egypt, and Syria, to name a few of the Arab Spring participants. Whether using ancient techniques or modern technology, the
driving force is the people behind it. Revolutions happen because of the
will of the people; the UGRR and the Internet are examples of platforms
used to facilitate those revolutions.

Because of the local networks, word of mouth communication, and
effective leaders throughout the Underground Railroad movement,
enslaved Africans learned about freedom, despite being unable to read or
write. Professor Siebert cites *The Firelands Pioneer* as his source for the
"grapevine telegraph." "Special signals, whispered conversations, passwords,
messages couched in figurative phrases, were the common modes of con-
veying information about underground passengers, or about parties in pursuit of fugitives." See the digital similarities in the language? In a letter to
Siebert dated August 2, 1896, conductor Alexander M. Ross said substa-

tions were identified by numbers and different names. For example, Meadville, Pennsylvania, was station 10 and the code word for the city of Detroit was midnight. Similarly, encrypted messages, passwords, and instant messages play an integral role on the Internet. A modern day Underground Railroad would be captured in video and pictures, shared with millions across the globe.

Leveraging word of mouth communication, information about the 1791 successful slave rebellion in San Domingo (now Haiti) spread to America, causing slave owners to panic. President George Washington gave Southern landowners money in advance in case a slave revolt took place. Slave owners' fears were nearly realized in 1800 when Gabriel Prosser attempted to lead a slave rebellion. Prosser sought to lead more than a thousand slaves in open rebellion, but bad weather (and leaked information to the governor of Virginia) ruined his plans.

When soldiers returned from the War of 1812, enslaved Africans heard about the land of freedom beyond the lakes, Canada. Queen Victoria had declared the Canadian territories free; this was the "promised land" mentioned in coded messages in song. As a historical side note, 1812 was the same year the city of Ripley, Ohio, was founded. Originally called Staunton, it was renamed after General Eleazar Wheelock Ripley, a distinguished officer that fought in the War of 1812. The town became a major stop on the Underground Railroad, due both to the large number of abolitionists living there and the close proximity to slave-state Kentucky on the other side of the Ohio River.

In his book *From Slavery to Freedom*, historian John Hope Franklin shares an account about an enslaved African man named George Boxley who planned an attack in Virginia in 1815. Another slave betrayed Boxley's confidence and revealed the plan, resulting in the deaths of several slaves (though Boxley managed to escape his imprisonment) and the banishment of several others from their respective plantations and communities. In 1821, a free Black man named Denmark Vesey also attempted to lead a revolt. He was betrayed, however, by two slaves opposed to his plan; Vesey was among the 35 people executed for the conspiracy. A clear lesson when fighting for change is to only announce the plan to certain people or keep it quiet until it is necessary to share; secrecy was what allowed the

Underground Railroad to be effective.

In 1831, an enslaved preacher named Nat Turner led the deadliest slave rebellion in American history. Turner and his rebels killed sixty Whites during the two-day revolt. In retaliation, nearly two hundred slaves and free Blacks were killed by militia, while Turner escaped capture until late October, and was formally executed the following month.

The Missouri Compromise in 1820, the Compromise of 1850, and the Kansas–Nebraska Act in 1854 set the stage for another prominent uprising in 1859, led by White abolitionist John Brown. The Missouri Compromise was struck to keep the number of slave and free states in balance; the South was seeking more political power, but Maine was added as a free state while Missouri entered as a slave state. Northerners were becoming more and more concerned about the "slave power" controlling the country's direction.

In 1845, the United States annexed Texas; this decisive act led to the Mexican–American War, fought from 1846 to 1848. Much of the opposition to the war came from those who were also opposed to slavery. A direct result of the war was the Compromise of 1850, a collection of bills that dictated where slavery would be allowed (for example, while the slave trade was banned in Washington, D.C., slavery itself was not, and California entered as a free state, but the territories of New Mexico and Utah would vote on the matter); the Fugitive Slave Act of 1850 was also introduced. This new legislation mandated that federal officials, in free and slave states alike, were to assist with the return of fugitive slaves; citizens were also held to the same standard. Individuals could lose property or their freedom as a result of non-compliance with the law; penalties were the same for aiding escaped slaves. As the enslaved were not citizens, anyone could lay claim to them; they did not warrant a jury trial, and they could not speak on the own behalf in court. Some Northerners were troubled by the updated legal codes, as it was clear that the South wanted to control the slave enterprise.

In 1854, additional pressure from the South led Congress to open the Western territories to slavery. Illinois Senator Stephen A. Douglas created the Kansas-Nebraska Act; rather than legislating whether Kansas and Nebraska would be free or slave states, citizens in those states would determine their status, a process known as popular sovereignty. As a result, pro-slavery advocates and abolitionists alike flooded into Kansas in the hope of swaying the vote to their respective sides, leading to numerous minor clashes between the two groups. This growing tension boiled over in Kansas in 1855. The city of Lawrence, Kansas was sacked by a pro-slavery posse led by the county sheriff. In reaction to this assault, abolitionist John Brown led an extremely violent revenge attack in Pottawatomie, killing five pro-slavery settlers. The series of skirmishes became known as Bleeding Kansas.

Around the same time of the Bleeding Kansas battles, John Brown received word that Massachusetts Senator Charles Sumner had been assaulted by South Carolina Representative Preston Brooks. On May 20, 1856, Sumner gave a passionate speech, calling what happened regarding Kansas a crime and incidentally spoke out against one of Brooks' relatives. Two days later, Brooks savagely attacked Sumner in the nearly-empty Senate chamber. Sumner was trapped under a desk, while a pistol-branding supporter of Brooks prevented anyone from interfering. In the South, Brooks was hailed as a hero; in the North, he was called a barbarian.

In 1858, Abraham Lincoln challenged the Senate seat occupied by Illinois Senator Stephen Douglas. They engaged in a series of seven debates throughout the state, with the main topic argued being slavery. Douglas supported the expansion of slavery, while Lincoln did not. Lincoln was accused of being an abolitionist, which he denied; Douglas, meanwhile, was chiefly interested in preserving popular sovereignty. The transcripts of the debates provide a wealth of research opportunities. While Douglas was reelected to Congress, Lincoln's increased exposure greatly helped his bid for the Presidency.

John Brown was an active abolitionist and Underground Railroad supporter, yet he wanted to do more. When a slave asked him for assistance, Brown and his men agreed to escort the fugitive more than twenty-five hundred miles to Canada. En route, Brown brought along several other slaves and one of his men killed a slave owner. Professor Wilbur Siebert believed this was the prelude to the raid Brown attempted to lead at Harpers Ferry in 1859. Brown had even asked Fredrick Douglass and Harriet Tubman to participate in the raid, yet both declined; ten years prior Brown had told Douglass he would start with a small group of men and then build his force by gaining slave supporters along the way, though Douglass told Brown that he wouldn't make it out alive. Brown did survive the failed raid, but was hung for leading the revolt. These are some of the circumstances when the Underground Railroad was operating at full steam. It was imperative for participants to innovate to address new developments.

Innovating freedom is what individuals, corporations, communities, civic and religious organizations, private and public institutions, government agencies, and any other organized entities must do. Innovation is not solely imitation; if you copy another company's strategy, that is not innovating. In William Taylor and Polly LaBarre's book, *Mavericks at Work*, the authors discuss how HBO adapts and switches gears and direction when others imitate them. HBO does not stand still long enough for others to comprehend its strategy. By the time some plantation overseers figured out a slave's plan, the slave had already changed it. The slaves had to be pioneers because they didn't have any idea what existed beyond the plantation.

In *The Tipping Point*, Malcolm Gladwell builds on Everett Rogers' research on innovation adoption. Gladwell analyzes the point where an idea becomes so popular it "tips" to the masses or into greater view. On the Underground Railroad, the "tipping point" occurred between the years of 1850-1860. It was during this period more Northern states publicly objected to the Fugitive Slave Law of 1850. Many Northerners didn't agree when free Blacks were fraudulently identified as fugitives and taken into slavery; they also resented being forced by law to help the slave catchers. Several states adopted personal liberty laws to avoid the national Fugitive Slave Law. During this decade, John Brown and other abolitionists were involved in the Bleeding Kansas battles, and the Missouri Compromise was eventually repealed. These events, in addition to some very public fugitive assists, greatly aggravated some slave owners.

This case happened in 1842, but it set off a chain of events culminating in the 1850s. A slave named Margaret Morgan was living in Pennsylvania, and her owner sent an agent by the name of Edward Prigg to retrieve her. However, Pennsylvania law at the time dictated that it was a felony to capture any Black for the purpose of restoring to slavery; this was contrary to the Fugitive Slave Law of 1793. Prigg was convicted, but he appealed to the Supreme Court. The Justices ruled the master had a right to reclaim his property, yet the state had no obligation to help him. It was a confusing decision, and led to the stricter Fugitive Slave Act of 1850.

Then in the 1850s, an Ohio farmer named John Van Zandt gave nine "colored" people a ride in his wagon. He told the authorities he did not know they were escaped slaves; however, as he had broken the federal Fugitive Slave Law, he was fined $1200. The amount left him bankrupt, and sent fear throughout the ranks of abolitionists and other anti-slavery citizens. In another case, George Latimer was a runaway slave who arrived in Boston with his wife; shortly thereafter, he was arrested and charged with larceny. The uproar over his arrest was so great, funds were secured to purchase his freedom and new personal liberty laws were adopted in Massachusetts.

During this same time period, one of the most historic court cases involving a slave was decided: the Dred Scott case. In summary, Scott lived with his master, an Army surgeon, at various posts in what is now the Midwest; when Scott returned home to Missouri, he petitioned for his freedom. A legal precedent existed that if a slave stayed in a free state beyond a certain length of time, they were to be considered free; Scott believed he had lived on free soil for such an extended period of time to qualify for freedom.

The Supreme Court ruled Scott was not a citizen. As a result, he could not bring a case against his master; his owner's rights superseded his own. The decision further contributed to the repealing of the Missouri Compromise. About the decision, Fergus Bordewich said this in his book *Bound for Canaan*: "When the Supreme Court issued its infamous Dred Scott decision in 1857, removing all existing territorial restrictions on slavery, members of the underground, and for that matter most of the North, expressed dismay, but in practice simply ignored it." In the state of Ohio, the decision was denounced.

The enslaved had no legal recourse and some took matters into their own hands. Abolitionists knew they needed to strengthen their ranks and improve their strategies for assisting passengers. Anti-slavery advocates even became more serious about protecting their freedom, given the courts' decisions. In addition, both the average cost per slave and the overall number of slaves had risen. By 1840, there were an estimated two and a half million slaves in the United States; by 1860, it was nearly four million. Some slaves sold for as little as $300, while a few commanded prices northward of $2000. Prices were primarily determined by the age, gender, and physical ability of the slave. Each person represented a considerable financial investment, and each time a slave was lost, bankruptcy loomed.

The Underground Railroad was an epidemic of deadly proportion for the slave power. Based on the characteristics of epidemics Gladwell describes, the UGRR demonstrates the conditions clearly. Epidemics are contagious: it was a small network with a huge effect, and its impact hit in a seemingly dramatic moment. In hindsight, it's easier to map out the trajectory of the events combining to make the Underground Railroad the revolutionary success it became.

SUMMARY

- Isaac Hopper was among the first conductors on the UGRR in the late eighteenth century.

- The UGRR was a leaderless movement, one without a central leader, headquarters, or centrally-coordinated effort.

- Harriet Tubman presents a classic leadership example worth further research.

- Tubman believed in the impossible, followed her intuition, didn't take credit for collective action, and helped disrupt the institution of slavery by freeing hundreds of enslaved Africans.

- The UGRR was a social network dependent upon word of mouth to lead some of the enslaved to freedom. The Internet facilitates social networks using word of mouth and social relationships to help individuals and countries embrace freedom.

- The UGRR was a local, organic, grassroots effort to unite a disconnected, diverse group of people to realize their goal of freedom for all involved.

- Internet websites are often created for local, organic, grassroots efforts to achieve a desired end.

- Some enslaved Africans fought for their freedom from the beginning, though sometimes the plans were leaked. Secrecy is key.

- The tipping point is when an idea "tips" into view.

- The years leading up to and between 1850-1860 were clearly a tipping point for the UGRR.

CHAPTER FOUR

Dr. Syb's Seven Elements of Innovation

"A spirit of innovation is generally the result of a selfish temper

and confined views. People will not look forward to posterity,

who never look backward to their ancestors."

EDMUND BURKE

The Underground Railroad addressed the problem of slavery in undetectable, immeasurable, and incalculable ways. In aggregation, the network circumvented the slave owner, the overseer, and even the slave catcher. It created just-in-time paths to freedom for the enslaved. Each escape was unique, even when fugitives followed a similar path as previous escapees. It was an effective and disruptive leaderless movement. It successfully used the desire for freedom to mobilize organically. Its location outside of the plantation, with some fugitives using swamps, rivers, or other unexpected means for escape, was disruptive and innovative.

Demonstrating the importance of diversity and cultivating diverse relationships, the UGRR allowed conductors, agents, friends, strangers, and enslaved to build credible reputations, leverage relationships, and connect

37

the unconnected. Never before seen strategies were employed. The level of coordination without a traditional organization was unprecedented. Over time, some preconceived notions about the fugitives' intellectual abilities were shattered. Fugitives faced the fear of the unknown, trusted their instincts, and demonstrated unimaginable bravery. All of these facts show that the UGRR was among the most effective, disruptive, and innovative networks in American history.

The experiences of UGRR participants also provide valuable and applicable lessons for contemporary leaders. As industry leaders continue to watch the implementation of innovations in the digital age, it is imperative for them to take chances. Waiting and wondering can have devastating effects on a corporation. Kodak was once the definitive leader of the camera industry; however, the shift to digital photography caught them flat-footed, and they filed for bankruptcy in January 2012. Encyclopedia Britannica was the gold standard for reference books, but the shift to digital formats left its position as the go-to encyclopedic resource vulnerable; first to Encarta, then to Wikipedia. There are numerous examples of companies standing still, failing to compete effectively with shifting markets. Focusing on adapting to change is a better use of one's time.

Based on the experiences of UGRR participants, companies would be wise to create and implement original ideas or remix old ones in unique ways. If one path is blocked, try a different one immediately. For the fugitives, it was literally a matter of life and death. Complaining and attempting to stifle competition doesn't work when you can't see, control, or comprehend the competition. Bragging is not a wise strategy either. Some really don't care about what you accomplished in the past; what you are doing in the present for a better future is more important. An escapee boasting about the journey would have destroyed the entire network, putting lives at risk and leaving hundreds of those still enslaved with no chance for their own escape.

The enslaved had to live in the moment and face reality. They were forced to hear hateful, discouraging, and devastating words from their captors. But some chose not to internalize those messages; it's not what you are called, it's what you answer to when called. Focusing on strengths, providing encouraging words, and offering the training employees need to contribute in the digital age is a strategy rooted in wisdom. Another lesson from the UGRR is to learn from the lessons of others. Stop paying full price for a lesson when others are still paying for the same one. When conductors were aiding fugitives, they had to utilize the experience of and information from others to avoid detection. It didn't matter who delivered the message; all were equal on the road to freedom.

Use your instincts and stop being so beholden to the past, compromising the present and obliterating the future. Channel *Good to Great* author Jim Collins by putting the right people in the right seat on the bus. Executives and managers may not be in the best position to lead innovation. The enslaved led, despite slave owners not believing the slaves could conceive a plan, let alone coordinate one. Assess the skills of your staff and find out who wants to innovate and put them in position to do so. Again, places outside of the existing system are where disruption occurs. These are just a few ways to apply the lessons from the Underground Railroad. Further analysis of the innovations on the UGRR will provide more.

It is not difficult to identify the innovative development and maintenance of the Underground Railroad; the approach and implementation of the network was innovative by its very design. What is innovative to one person may be considered antiquated by another; innovation should not only be seen in the eye of the innovator.

A system, framework, or blueprint is needed to better study innovation. What are the characteristics of innovation? What do innovators have in common? How is the product or service innovative? Recall from chapter one, Dr. Syb's Seven Elements of Innovation are: problem, principle, purpose, perspective, pioneering, passion, and play. Applying each one to assess the effort and impact of the UGRR is an innovative approach to analyze the implementation of creativity.

1. Problem

Identifying a problem is a key component in innovation. Innovators are clever enough to see the problem and savvy enough to solve it. The enslaved did not have restrictive rules and guidelines inhibiting their ability to think; in many ways, not having a formal education helped some slaves.

Within the educational system, people sometimes learn more about fear than about faith, and trying to teach a scared person not to fear is nearly impossible; experience is the best way. In *Mavericks at Work*, William C. Taylor and Polly LaBarre share this insight from Arkadi Kuhlmann, founder of ING Direct USA, a bank focused on savers instead of investors:

> "If you want to renew and re-energize an industry…don't hire people from that industry. You've got to untrain them and then retrain them. I'd rather hire a jazz musician, a dancer or a captain in the Israeli army. They can learn about banking. It's much harder for bankers to unlearn their bad habits. They're trapped by the past. Remember, resurrection has only worked once in history."

Internalize and apply Kuhlmann's quote. Many industries are struggling due to CEO stubbornness; it's time to change. Some enslaved Africans did not have such entrenched views. They were flexible, allowing them to adapt to a circumstance, making their behavior disruptive, unpredictable, and often exactly what they needed to make it to the next safe place. Conductors and agents on the UGRR were willing to sacrifice all they had. Those new on the UGRR did not want to fail and they were bold (or scared) enough to try new routes, paths, or ideas. Some American companies and institutions can learn important lessons from their bravery.

Being owned by another human being is illegal and immoral. The enslaved did not come to America seeking the American Dream; they were brought to help White slave owners achieve a "privileged" dream. Sociologist John Ogbu calls this group, "involuntary minorities."

2. Principle

A principle is grounded in integrity, providing a solid foundation upon which to build ideas. It's the platform for embarking on the journey. Freedom is an exemplary principle, well worth innovating to preserve and protect. Why is the innovation needed? Is it purely for profit? Who will benefit from its creation? Will those who need it most have access to it? How will it contribute to society at large? These are just a few of the questions to consider.

Abolitionists and anti-slavery supporters fought for freedom, in both practice and principle. The architects of democracy in America created the Declaration of Independence with these words:

> "We hold these truths to be self-evident, that all men are created equal, that they are endowed by their Creator with certain unalienable Rights, that among these are Life, Liberty and the pursuit of Happiness."

It's interesting the founding fathers used the phrase "the pursuit of happiness." We have the right to chase happiness, but there's no guarantee it will or can be caught. The freedom to function as a contributing citizen in society should never be compromised, yet for an extended period, it was. The principle in this democratic society is crystal clear: all Americans should be free.

Indiana abolitionist Levi Coffin, considered by some to be an unofficial leader on the Underground Railroad, agreed with helping enslaved Africans on the run. However, he did not agree with those who went to the south and encouraged escapes; Coffin believed in the principle of freedom. He did not seek fugitives; they found him. He had a spiritual conviction to the principle of freedom: Coffin felt it was his calling to help those in need.

3.Purpose

Purpose pertains to direction, so one of the first questions to be asked is: what is the purpose for innovating? In other words, what is the goal? In which direction are you heading and why? What is the desired end? The enslaved wanted to be recognized as human beings. They wanted access to information, the right to participate in the political process, and the ability to manage their own lives. The purpose was to move out of their current position of darkness and into the light of freedom. Innovation helped them realize their purpose moving forward to achieve a collective victory.

As an innovation, the UGRR formed to fulfill a purpose. Innovation should be intentional, purposeful; for example, the Underground Railroad formed to fulfill a specific purpose. The fugitives who made it to freedom had a purpose to remember. The enslaved should be defined by their purpose, not by their circumstance. Often, the enslaved are historically misrepresented as grotesque caricatures, as demonstrated in the documentary *Ethnic Notions*. In modern times, some jokingly call each other slaves as it pertains to work and to having a work ethic; this is an insult to the enslaved. Their workday began before the sun rose and ended long after the moon appeared. They worked pregnant, deathly ill, maimed, or crippled. Their legacy should be revered, not rejected or relegated to a historical footnote. Many of the enslaved answered the call to action by aiding fugitives, escaping in the night, distracting an overseer, sharing information, or performing the task required to keep the UGRR trains running.

Based on the remarkable way the enslaved realized their purpose, there really aren't any viable excuses for contemporary generations not to succeed. Innovation is always an option, but should not be optional. The enslaved not only innovated with purpose, they implemented change on purpose. This is part of the reason why the UGRR was so effective: each participant understood their position and played it.

4. Perspective

Innovation is a matter of believing in what cannot be seen. Fundamentally, it involves the ability to change one's perspective and/or attitude to accept and facilitate change. Whether the glass is half full or half empty, whether it's a chance or a challenge, a dead-end or a new beginning, an individual's perspective is among the most powerful weapons in their control. It is really a matter of mindset.

The late Apple founder Steve Jobs saw products the consumer would need (or believe they needed) before the market demanded them. Jobs convinced engineers to create the impossible. This is similar to the experiences of some gamers; their thought process eliminates real and imagined obstacles. It frees participants to create without fear or penalty. Being able to envision what does not exist is an invaluable skill unique to a chosen few.

Mental flexibility is not optional in the digital age. Americans must be able to adjust their mindset and to do it quickly as the manufacturing age disappears and the network age connects us globally. In *The World is Flat,*

New York Times journalist Thomas Friedman talks about how the Internet connects all countries, "flattening" the world. Because there is greater access to an international network, Friedman implores his readers to choose jobs that cannot be outsourced or handled by a computer. The other option is to change one's perspective in order to innovate pioneering solutions, as some of the enslaved chose to do on the UGRR.

5. Pioneering

Whether an innovation is new or remixed, the product or service should be original. Does the product or service already exist? If so, how can we build upon, extend, or improve it? How does the new idea build on existing knowledge? Will this innovation explore uncharted territory? What precedent can this product set? Many will argue there is nothing new under the sun. However, in days past and in days to come innovation will continue.

The Underground Railroad was a pioneering experiment. The enslaved didn't have maps, and global positioning systems were beyond their imaginations. Many could not speak English. They created a new culture, a new set of norms, a new way of life. They had to innovate as they went. They created new codes, routes, and customs.

The fugitives who left the plantation were remarkable. But their ingenuity was only original for so long; they had to keep innovating depending on the circumstance they faced. They couldn't use the same escape route, plan, or disguise. For example, consider the way William and Ellen Craft escaped the chains of slavery: Ellen disguised herself as a man, her right arm in a sling and a cane in her left hand, dependent on her husband who posed as her servant. Ellen's White father had raped her Black mother, producing a child with a pale complexion; it was this fair skin that allowed Ellen to pass as White. According to Marcia Alesan Dawkins in *Clearly Invisible: Racial Passing and the Color of Cultural Identity*, one definition of passing "refers to the means by which nonwhite people represent themselves as white." This is the origin of the one-drop rule: if a person was known to have one drop of African blood, they were classified as Black. F. James Davis provides great insight on this issue in his book *Who is Black?*; another insightful book on the topic is *The Color Complex: The Politics of*

Skin Color in a New Millennium by Kathy Russell, Midge Wilson, and Ronald Hall. The Craft's idea to have Ellen pass as White to secure her freedom was creative; ultimately, the Crafts made it to England, making their innovation a success.

Another pioneering act involved the way some slaves communicated with each other. Following Nat Turner's unsuccessful slave insurrection in Virginia in 1831, slaves were forbidden to meet. Remember, Turner was a preacher who led a rebellion that killed roughly sixty Whites in a day and a half. After the attack, it was illegal for more than two slaves to talk to each other so they invented a new way to share information. When they viewed a body at a funeral, the bereaved or other appointed person shared the necessary details regarding an escape plan. The enslaved Africans contributed financially to escape efforts by paying dues to private groups using numbers instead of their names. Their actions showed their commitment, courage, and passion.

6. Passion

Passion is the indescribable and indomitable force leading to innovative action. It compels innovators to stay up for days at a time, focused entirely on the task at hand. The success of an innovation can be assessed based on the extent of passion and determination of the innovator. On the UGRR, those who placed their lives and livelihoods on the line to act as conductors, guides, and stationmasters, whose homes were used as safe places, were passionate to say the least.

In *Bound for Canaan*, Fergus Bordewich describes abolitionist Gerrit Smith as a thirty-something philanthropist with nothing to prove but a whole lot to give. Smith was huge in stature with enough passion to fill his frame. He suffered bouts with depression yet he still made significant contributions to "keep the trains running" on the UGRR. His passion to help the enslaved began in childhood when his father forced him to work with them. The experience of walking in another man's shoes changed him.

Gerrit Smith offered his palatial New York estate as a meeting place for the anti-slavery society, in addition to it being a refuge for fugitive slaves. He also shared other resources. He was known to keep large amounts of money on his desk to help anyone in need. Before he died, Smith made a sizeable donation to Howard University, a historically Black university in Washington, D.C. His actions were disruptive, helping to change the course of history.

7. Play

Although play is a lighter concept and may seem inappropriate in a discussion about the Underground Railroad, it is relevant when considering innovation as a concept. Play may involve fun, strategy and collaboration. How does the innovation create an opportunity for consumers to engage in an enjoyable experience? How does it encourage collaboration? Does the innovation promote creative thinking? Does the innovation depend on rules or accomplishing an end goal?

In his 2010 presentation at the TED (Technology, Entertainment, Design) conference, Princeton dropout Seth Priebatsch and partner in SCVNGR, a company using location based metrics to improve commerce, talks about how the previous decade was about the social graph, spawning social media giants like Facebook and Twitter. Priebatsch predicts the next decade will focus on game dynamics, sharing four of them. They include an appointment dynamic, "leveling up," attaining status and influence, and realizing a common purpose through communal discovery.

Fugitives had to travel during certain times of day. They moved from one safe place to the next, thus "leveling up" as they made it closer to their destination. The status and influence of conductors and agents grew as they helped more fugitives to safety. Finally, there was a common goal in the end: freedom for the slaves, representing their communal discovery.

When fugitives escaped they employed strategy and deception. The enslaved Africans could not tell the master or certain other slaves his/her plan. They had to "play" dumb. Some pretended they couldn't read. Others appeared to be unable to understand English. Some of the spies during the Civil War were enslaved persons who were assumed to be ignorant. The charade helped save the lives of millions of people.

In several prominent cases in the twenty-first century, entrepreneurs were just playing around when they came up with a new idea. They are

DR. SYB'S SEVEN ELEMENTS OF INNOVATION

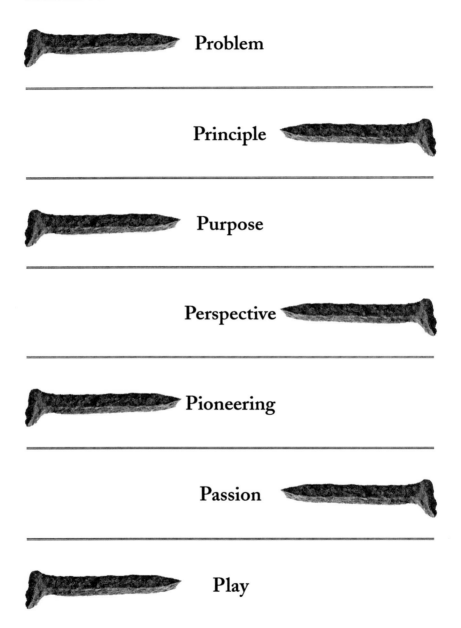

Problem

Principle

Purpose

Perspective

Pioneering

Passion

Play

passionate people with or without college degrees who have a great time tinkering with their hobbies and interests. The co-creator of Twitter, Evan Williams was "twittering" with a friend when they created the mega micro-blogging site. Now in 140 characters or less revolutions have been revealed, earthquakes have been reported, and a vice presidential candidate was announced. Other digital innovations come to mind such as Angry Birds, Pinterest, and Aurasma. Each innovator was just playing around or just trying to help people use technology in order to find a solution to a problem even if the problem was boredom.

To summarize, innovation involves purpose, passion, principle, a problem, pioneering, play, and perspective. Throughout this book, each component's role in innovating freedom will be explored using the UGRR comparatively with contemporary times. This work demonstrates how the enslaved African's journey into the unknown parallels the pilgrimage of many into cyberspace and doing business in the knowledge and information age. Both the enslaved and workers were and are often passengers on a train trying to take control of their destiny.

SUMMARY

- The Underground Railroad formed to address the legalized system of slavery.
- Companies can learn valuable lessons from the experiences of the enslaved and their supporters on the UGRR.
- Adaptability and flexibility were imperative on the UGRR.
- Dr. Syb's Seven Elements of Innovation are: problem, principle, purpose, perspective, pioneering, passion, and play.
- What is the problem to be solved?
- Upon what foundational principle does the new or remixed idea stand?
- What is the desired end or purpose, and in what direction does one need to go to get there?
- What is the mindset surrounding the innovative initiative? From what perspective is it being approached?
- Does the product or service already exist? How will the idea be pioneering, unique, "a first," or set a precedent?
- What is the driving force behind the innovation or idea? Where does the passion lie?
- How does the idea or innovation provide consumers with an opportunity to

CHAPTER FIVE

Problem

"Sometimes the messiest approach is the wisest."

JAMES SUROWIECKI

On the UGRR there was no shortage of problems in need of solutions. The legal yet unethical and inconceivable system of enslavement existed. Human beings were being held in bondage against their will without rights to legally fight the injustice. A minority of people in power had manipulated the system to favor the few at the expense of many. Voices to challenge the immoral basis for slavery were often ignored or silenced. If a fugitive attempted to escape unsuccessfully, he was branded, beaten and/or buried. Those who attempted to aid a fugitive could be fined, jailed or killed. Reason, rationality and responsibility to humanity were the pink elephants in the room. And these are just a few of the problems created by the inhumane institution.

For enslaved Africans, one of the most pressing issues was physical bondage. Some literally worked with chains attached, while others were maimed for straying to far across the plantation property line. Personal freedom did not exist to use the restroom, to bathe or to engage in intimate relationships. After all, the enslaved were often called animals to dehumanize and depersonalize them. They were not allowed to marry like the civilized citizens who enslaved them. During slavery, "animal" abuse was a protected right. It was perfectly acceptable to kick, punch, slap or discipline enslaved property.

Former slave turned abolitionist, Frederick Douglass described how an overseer named Mr. Gore killed a slave named Demby. Gore believed he had to set an example. Demby disrespected Gore by defending himself. Gore didn't let any enslaved Africans get away with anything. He felt if one survived and told the others, the slaves could try to assert their power. Gore killed Demby in front of the other slaves without regret or remorse. With crushing overseers like Gore it was nearly impossible for slaves to come together to coordinate a plan to escape yet many did. Slavery for all practical purposes was a labyrinth with no end.

Ownership was another problem for enslaved Africans. Being identified as property posed numerous dilemmas. The First Amendment to the United States Constitution protected the rights of American citizens. Considered property, the enslaved were not citizens. Americans had the right to free speech, to practice religion, to a free press, to assemble and to petition the government. Even citizens opposing slavery had their rights compromised. The House of Representatives created the gag rule to prohibit anti-slavery discussions. It was seemingly a hopeless situation. Human beings held against their will without rights or recourse.

Abruptly switching gears to the notion of ownership and privacy in the digital age it was clear the enslaved didn't have rights or a voice regarding these issues. Their privacy was violated daily. Yet, hundreds of years later, citizens voluntarily yield private space on an international platform. Definitions of privacy vary. It is an individual decision. However, information from birth, divorce, death, and property records to voter registration is accessible to the public. When people had to physically go to a building to obtain public records, access was limited to those in the area. However, with the advent of the Web more data can be retrieved online. In addition, Facebook has a wealth of data willingly provided by the user, including birthdates, political position, religion, even place of birth. And with sites like Amazon storing information about individual purchases, the aggregated searchable data is substantive. In the digital age, data is currency.

These facts are not shared to cause alarm but to raise awareness. With so much information so readily accessible, the "who owns what" question is critical. The most accurate answer is "it depends." A consumer pays hundreds if not thousands of dollars to purchase songs from iTunes can he/she transfer music to loved ones upon death? Actor Bruce Willis allegedly raised this issue. The answer to this question is in the user agreement. And based on reviews of the document, the answer is no. The situation should cause one to assess and appropriate digital assets ahead of time. Some people have included their digital holdings in their will along with their passwords so loved ones can close and/or manage their virtual accounts.

Here's another question for discussion, who owns a photograph? Again, the answer is it depends. In most cases, the person who presses the button owns the picture. Meaning, when asking a stranger to take a picture with your camera, the stranger owns the photo. The primary exception to this rule involves contracted work. Read the fine print. Some photographers could have joint ownership of wedding pictures for example. When you pay for pictures make sure you have sole ownership. The same holds true when publishing pictures online. Certain social networks may be able to access and use your photos for commercial and/or non-commercial endeavors. This means if you are not compensated initially for the post, you may watch others make money from your work. Instead of reading the fine print, scroll the lengthy text and read the user agreement.

Even if you own the photographs, videos and other content it can often be accessed and used by third parties. If you play games through a website like Facebook, the application developer may be granted access to the information you willingly provided for commercial gain by selling it to advertisers. On some sites, you can change your privacy settings to prohibit these types of transactions. This information may seem tangential. It is connected to the past as America continues to address ownership, access and economic issues.

Making a profit from the masses by leveraging power and control is not new. The enslaved were often physically branded letting their owners know who they were. This process of burning an indelible mark into human flesh also made it easier for slave owners to recover their missing property. And yes they used the same branding irons for their cattle. In the digital age, branding is a form of tagging. Tagging in modern society used to refer primarily to graffiti. Online tagging means putting a person's name on a picture or a post. This identification follows the person all over the web and is searchable since the person has been identified. Tagging is a brand or a mark linking one to the published information about the individual.

Graffiti is a way to mark one's territory and it can be considered an outside attack on an existing system. In *The Pirate's Dilemma*, Matt Mason provides several examples of intense tagging. He used the graffiti in New York as an example of youth expression in public space. On the Internet, your tag, whether it's on photos or words to describe you will follow you virtually forever. Mason argues the graffiti "blowback" was a rebellion against the privatization of common space. Imagine that, young people rebelling against the establishment because they felt their independence was compromised. This is exactly what some enslaved Africans did more than a century ago.

Taking yet another virtual leap making comparisons between the period of enslavement and the digital age, some school systems have embedded tracking mechanisms into student identification cards. It's a controversial move yet corporations stand to make considerable profits from the Radio Frequency Identification Device (RFID). In a familiar turn, the RFID chips are also used in livestock just like branding was used for the enslaved and cattle. The device allows teachers to take attendance without saying a word. While in school, the child's whereabouts would always be known. With the addition of the RFID chips, tagging may become more common off line than it is online.

Whether in the past or in the present, major stakeholders invade privacy to make billions. Ironically, today the difference is many citizens in the twenty-first century are complicit providing data for companies to sell, allowing children to be monitored for safety reasons and turning a blind eye to the imposition. It's a classic debate between George Orwell's book *1984* and Aldous Huxley's book *A Brave New World* colliding with Neil Postman's *Amusing Ourselves to Death* yet most people don't understand the joke let alone the punch line. At least the enslaved knew their rights, humanity and conscience were being violated and many fled in protest catching a ride on the UGRR to protest the injustice.

Being in physical bondage, lacking government access, having one's privacy invaded and dealing with the issue of ownership made way for another pressing challenge for enslaved Africans, access to education. In his biography, Frederick Douglass shared his experience as an enslaved African. In it he discussed how the enslaved were murdered or severely injured for learning how to read and write. Even those who taught the enslaved how to read could be punished. It was an intentional effort to limit and to control the intellectual capabilities of the captives. The slave owners believed if they could control the thoughts of the enslaved, the enslaved would be content with their circumstance. Dominating the enslaved person's perspective helped keep the slave owner empowered. In order to escape, the enslaved had to envision a different reality.

Returning to the comparisons between the UGRR and the Internet, the Internet helps connect people globally and allows a common cause to become an international collaboration instantaneously. About the digital age New York University Professor Clay Shirky said, a lot of the obstacles hampering the ability of groups to form and to coordinate have been eliminated online. UGRR conductor Harriet Tubman didn't have the Internet or the World Wide Web as a network. She participated in a human network to solve a problem. And like the modern day Internet, the Underground Railroad was an open source network.

On some websites anyone can use, copy, and share certain software, content, music, etc. as long as they honor the wishes of the content provider and/or the community. In the pure open source space, the main rule is to create something someone else can use freely. In the words of Erik Qualman, creator of the world's most popular social media video, the Social Media Revolution, and author of *Digital Leader: 5 Simple Keys to Success and Influence,* open source allows people to fail forward, fail fast, and fail better. This explains how some fugitives left the plantations walking alone until they unintentionally ended up using part of the UGRR. It was an open source, living, expanding and changing network. Agents would meet passengers sending them to various stops. Those depots were adjusted en route based on the safety of the location. Anyone could intervene to help a "friend."

On the UGRR, fugitives did not know which homes or places were safe. They had to trust strangers to lead them from one stop to the next.

The sole responsibility of certain participants on the route was to watch for slave catchers and slave owners. The fugitives' fate often depended on the competence of the conductors and agents. In order to travel through the freedom network, fugitives had to leave everything behind from their belongings to their beloved. Some refused to do so and were caught as a result. Imagine that, the present was compromised as they tried to drag their past into the future. Catch the wisdom as it flows.

Those who chose to escape couldn't think the same way. They couldn't act the same way. They had to re-invent themselves in order to solve the problem. The switch to the digital age is forcing many to do the same. See the parallels. In order to solve the problem, the enslaved had to change. As the computer continues to displace workers by providing information and intelligence, fate will force others to recognize the problem and innovate solutions to solve it. Many companies are not willing to shift from the factory worker to the knowledge worker paradigm. Like some slaves, they refuse to leave some things from the past behind in order to prepare for a better future.

Ironically, part of the problem with the contemporary capitalist system is some people still don't believe they are free. They are shackled by a corporate mindset not realizing the power of the technological tools at their fingertips. Some people are happiest being told what to do. They are cogs in the wheel. They drank all of the Kool-Aid and do not enjoy thinking independently. Meaning, they accept what they've been taught and told instead of seeking truth on their own. At least the fugitives and their UGRR supporters were brave enough to revolt to change the system and to fight for freedom.

The enslavement problem demanded social innovation. According to Jane McGonigal in her book *Reality is Broken: Why Games Make Us Better and How They Can Change the World*, social innovation "means applying entrepreneurial ways of thinking and working to solve social problems that are ordinarily tackled by governments or by relief and aid agencies." Without government assistance, the abolitionists and the enslaved had to work together on the UGRR. Indeed, they operated as social innovators. McGonigal argues social innovation in gaming can and should play an instrumental role in improving society as a whole.

To support her premise, McGonigal offers fourteen ways to fix reality through gaming. Fix number fourteen is "Reality is stuck in the present. Games help us imagine and invent the future together." EVOKE is a game created for the World Bank Institute to empower young people, especially in Africa, to address the most pressing problems worldwide. The scenario involves a group of stealth social innovators who, like superheroes, find solutions to problems. An "evoke" is "an urgent call to innovation." In some parts of Africa, innovation is the only option. The superheroes are to respond to a crisis set ten years in the future but they gather real world information and help local communities in reality. This is what took place on the UGRR. When some enslaved Africans and their supporters encountered a crisis they innovated a solution.

McGonigal shares the work of Erik Hersman, a technologist and editor for the blog AfriGadget. She provides real examples of African ingenuity reminiscent of ideas implemented by the enslaved more than a century ago. "A Malawian boy creates a windmill from old bicycle parts and sheet metal. A Kenyan man fabricates welding machines from scrap metal, wood, and copper wire. An Ethiopian entrepreneur makes coffee machines from old mortar shells." With more than 2.5 million views on You Tube, a video about 15 year old Kelvin Doe, a self taught engineer from Sierra Leone confirms the heritage of innovation in Africa continues. Doe literally uses things he finds in the trash to create his future. He's built batteries, generators and even a radio transmitter to become a disc jockey. This type of innovation and creativity to solve problems was ever-present on the UGRR. It occurred most often when the fugitives were brave enough to think and to help create their own destinies. Innovation really happened on demand.

Some of life's most pressing problems will be solved on demand. Malcolm Gladwell believes some issues are best resolved in a "blink." In the book *Blink*, he argues split second decisions can be as, if not more effective than data-laden ones. The enslaved had to depend on what was in front of them. The skills they possessed when they arrived in America and the ones they learned from laboring were useful. Gladwell believes understanding is often more important than knowledge. The enslaved were forced to assess and to understand a situation without a lot of data. The lack of knowledge helped to mitigate the fear of the unknown.

Although some fugitives successfully left the plantation and reached a safe house, they still had problems to solve. At times, slave catchers were hot on their trails and the fugitives had to conceal their identities and locations any way they could. Charles Gilbert was a slave in Virginia. His owner was in the process of selling him to the "deep" South when Gilbert paid a captain on a steamer for a ride to freedom. On his journey, he had to hide in a tree, under a floor, and even disguise himself as a woman to avoid capture. Escapees couldn't go back so they had to go forward. Remaining in their dire situations wasn't an option. Standing still could have led to a fugitive's capture and death. The stakes aren't as high in the virtual world yet so many companies and individuals in the digital age would greatly benefit from researching the innovations created on the UGRR to preserve and to protect freedom.

The ability to share information virtually has forced the world to collectively evaluate the notions of freedom, democracy, and access. In short, during slavery the battle was over control, political power, and participation. The issues are the same in the digital age. Whether the issue is net neutrality, who owns the access portals to the web, privacy and security, or whether it should be legal for Google to take pictures of every neighborhood in the US and post them online, the "who owns what" fight may never end. Because of the Internet, anyone with access can potentially produce anything so the large companies are no longer in control of setting prices, content, or making far-reaching decisions. The gatekeepers no longer control the gate. This is the same impact the UGRR had on the institution of slavery. It provided access to freedom. The UGRR network took the power out of the hands of the slave owners and gave enslaved Africans a chance.

The Internet allows active participation. Imagine how hard it was for the once enslaved to function freely once they were off the plantation. It might take some unimaginable event to wake Americans up to realize this is the closest people have been to true freedom due to the digital age. Certain people are no longer the only ones with access. During "Manifest Destiny", the proposed expansion in America and beyond after the acquisition of Texas, did not include minorities, women, or poor people. The Internet, unlike Manifest Destiny, provides an opportunity for many more players.

The capitalist system in the 1800s did not encourage people to work together. It encouraged individualism. Individualism is the Eurocentric approach. Collectivism is an Afrocentric approach. This is part of the reason why some American companies are having trouble collaborating globally. It follows the individualistic model. The late Rev. Dr. Martin Luther King, Jr. once said, America's arrogance and greed would be the death of her. His words are worthy of deeper thought and reflection. Just because some refuse to say or acknowledge the obvious doesn't mean the reality isn't true. It's the proverbial bull in the China shop. A bull runs through breaking up everything in its path and never turns around to see the damage. Therefore, to the bull, the broken glass doesn't exist.

Freedom is a necessity in the digital information age. It was a necessity for the enslaved. The UGRR formed to address the dire situation. In the *Wealth of Networks,* Harvard University Professor Yochai Benkler says because of the Internet groups lacking power are less likely to be manipulated by a privileged class. The Internet allows power not only to be decentralized but also to be distributed. Greater access equals more opportunities for entrepreneurial endeavors. In other words, people are sharing; some because they have no other choice and others because they choose to do so. It's a matter of by fate or by force. Again, some of the enslaved escaped by choice others by fate.

Benkler and many others state the obvious—as power and control shift, more people will benefit. In the words of Gomer Pyle, "GOLLLY, you've got to be kidding me?" More people who need information now have direct access to it. The key is to help them find it and understand it. Part of the financial future lies in organizing and indexing information as Jeff Jarvis asserts in *What Would Google Do?* Google helps people find information. They're in the search business. Conductors and scouts along the Underground Railroad had to search for safe routes. Jarvis also talks about creating platforms, doing what you do best and linking to the rest, and knowing what business you are in now that the world has changed. The UGRR was an open source network in the freedom business assisting fugitive escapes in disruptive, effective and innovative ways.

There is so much to be gained from the experiences of the participants on the UGRR. The value of leveraging relationships is paramount. Face to face interaction remains invaluable. Fugitives on the UGRR encountered strangers, treating each person in a civil manner as a brother, a sister and/or a friend proved beneficial. In an essay about civility and social media for *Haternation: How Incivility and Racism Are Dividing Us* edited by Neil Foote, I used Yale University Law Professor Stephen L. Carter's definition of civility. He says it is the sum of sacrifices we are called to make for the sake of living together. Civility is a matter of morality. It is a personal responsibility accepted to ensure each passenger in the journey of life is afforded respect. It's a way to handle disagreements through intentional dialogue. Carter uses examples from the Civil Rights Movement and the UGRR to strengthen his position. This work does the same linking innovation to a historic network.

Viewing others as equals made the UGRR function more effectively. It also made the network disruptive because slave owners could not identify the abolitionists or the fugitives. Fugitives could appear to be free Blacks. Not belittling or underestimating the enslaved Africans abilities helped UGRR participants. The responsibility was balanced and every intellectual resource was used to help solve problems. Some decisions must be made immediately. Companies and individuals can learn from the unpredictable experiences of the enslaved.

Innovation solves a problem. The problem may be an injustice, an imbalance, or an imposition. The UGRR network solved a problem for some enslaved Africans by providing a route to their freedom. The impact of the UGRR is often overlooked. It often takes at least a century to realize the true impact of a revolutionary innovation. Books are still being written about the impact of Gutenberg's printing press. Part of the story surrounding the Internet may be written in real-time yet to capture its historical significance will take much longer. For now many leaders continue to underestimate the power, reach and relevance of the virtual world. This blindspot is preventing many from seeing real problems because they are busy imagining ones that don't exist. In the digital age, innovation is helping the world collaborate, communicate, and create community as the UGRR did in the nineteenth century.

SUMMARY

- Problems to be addressed were ever-present during the legalized system of bondage.

- The enslaved Africans faced physical bondage, the ability of slave owners to own slaves as defined by law and their inability to petition the government for freedom.

- In an analogous way enslaved Africans were like pieces of data on the Internet, subject to ownership by anyone.

- The enslaved were branded, marked like cattle in modern times it can be compared to the permanence of branding online and tagging on and off line.

- Who owns data? It depends.

- Graffiti is a way for youth to create public space in a privatized world.

- For some, capitalism compromises conscience.

- The open source movement allows for sharing, copying and collaboration on the Internet.

- The UGRR facilitated open source escapes for some enslaved Africans.

- The enslaved and their UGRR supporters were social innovators, people thinking outside of the box to solve the problems governments failed to address.

- Split second decisions are sometimes most effective.

- The Internet forces the U.S. to face the issues of freedom, democracy, access and boundaries like the UGRR did centuries ago.

CHAPTER SIX

Principle

"Moderation in temper is always a virtue;

but moderation in principle is always a vice."

THOMAS PAINE

The Underground Railroad is an example of an effective network grounded firmly on the principle of freedom. It had a solid foundation upon which to grow and to extend. Fundamentally, it was a person-to-person escape network. Similarly, the Internet's growth and development often depends on peer-to-peer efforts. Enslaved Africans encountered strangers who passed them on to the next agent along their journey to freedom. Each agent shared their wisdom by knowing where the slave catchers and safe houses were. The UGRR was an "open source" operation, free of structural and authoritative constraints, depending on collaboration, connection, and community. The online community participates in file, code, information, time, and other forms of sharing. These relationships often lead to innovative outcomes.

In the virtual age, Harvard's Yochai Benkler explains how individuals have a great deal more to give online. He calls it their "extra capacity." In the "free" online environment, users can share more. Because people work together, they create much more than they could individually. The Underground Railroad was an intricate network with "extra capacity." Because of the people who participated by choice as well as by fate, the "extra" effort and outlets were often maximized. One beneficiary of this "extra capacity" was Josiah Henson, a prominent slave who made it to freedom. It is believed Harriet Beecher Stowe used his life as the basis for her main character in the book *Uncle Tom's Cabin*.

Henson knew his mother and father growing up until his father had a run-in with the man who owned Henson's mother. Apparently, the owner had tried to rape her, which sent his father into an understandable rage. His father lost his ear in the altercation, and was later sold off. Shortly thereafter, Henson and the rest of his family were put up for auction. Henson's mother was sold to a man named Isaac Riley; Henson was initially sold to Riley's neighbor, but was eventually sold to Riley as well. After watching the horrors his father experienced, Henson became a model, loyal slave. Through the years, he was rewarded with greater freedom and greater responsibilities than some other slaves. Henson was a man who lived on principles in spite of his circumstances.

Henson, along with his wife and children, were eventually given to Isaac Riley's brother, Amos. Henson began working to purchase his family's freedom, but was swindled by his former owner. This was a common practice by slave owners: telling the enslaved to work extra jobs to buy their freedom, then stealing it. This encounter profoundly changed Henson; he was no longer just a dutiful slave. It was his "tipping point." This act of betrayal led Henson to flee before his family could be sold once again.

Like so many other fugitives, Henson made his escape via the Ohio River. It was a long and perilous journey, but the Hensons eventually made it to Canada. His escape was facilitated by the "extra capacity" on the UGRR. Ultimately, Henson established the Dawn Settlement in Canada. The Quakers helped him to open a vocational school and sawmill. In spite of his liberty being compromised, his trust betrayed, and his life nearly lost, Henson exhibited sound principles throughout his innovative journey.

In Taylor and LaBarre's *Mavericks at Work: Why the Most Original Minds in Business Win*, it is clear principle matters. Their very first chapter, "Not Just a Company, a Cause: Strategy as Advocacy," sets the tone for their work. Texas-based advertising executive Roy Spence told the two that Southwest Airlines is in the freedom business, saying "Business strategies change. Market positioning changes. But purpose does not change. Everybody at Southwest is a freedom fighter." Spence called it "purpose". Purpose is one of Dr. Syb's Seven Elements of Innovation, which will be discussed in Chapter 7. However, freedom isn't just a direction or a destination; it's an unchanging principle. On the Underground Railroad, conductors and routes changed, but the reason for helping slaves escape never changed: they valued freedom for all Americans, even the enslaved.

Why would a group of people, strangers even, risk their lives for each other? Many did it because they believed in freedom. Others did not want the laws enacted to control the enslaved Africans to negatively affect their lives. To be clear, there were abolitionists who wanted slavery abolished immediately. Many didn't mind free Blacks living in their communities. Also, some Southern slaveholders did not realize the number of Whites who did not support the peculiar institution. They just didn't want the "absolute power" of the South to set the policy for the entire country.

Some abolitionists as well as enslaved Africans were innovators. They were the first ones to explore paths to freedom. Free Blacks were prominent members of this group, setting up communities within free territories. Researcher Wilbur Siebert learned that the colored people of Greenwich, New Jersey; the Stewart Settlement of Jackson County, Ohio; the Upper and Lower Camps, Brown County, Ohio; and the Colored Settlement, Hamilton County, Indiana were active links on the UGRR. Each conductor and agent maximized his or her strength and outsourced the rest. It was an intelligent design further strengthening the UGRR. Focusing on weaknesses made them weak. The "extra capacity" in the form of free Blacks helped facilitate escapes. They wanted freedom for all and to reunite with their families and to help others do the same. It was an effective strategy, especially since fugitives could more easily blend in at free Black settlements.

Some Blacks were free at birth in America. Some remained free upon arrival, others paid for their freedom, some were freed upon their owner's death, and some were rewarded with their freedom for good service. In Ann Hagedorn's *Beyond the River*, she discusses how the Gist Settlement emerged. Nearly 1,000 slaves were freed upon their owner Samuel Gist's death in 1818, moving from Virginia and settling in Ohio, not too far from Ripley.

Some slaveholders did not want their slaves interacting with freed Blacks. In 1806, Virginia passed a law requiring freed slaves to leave the state within one year of their emancipation or face re-enslavement. Free Blacks could not co-exist with slaves. At times, innovators cannot thrive with members in the early and late majority or laggard groups. The fears of the latter group frustrate the faith of the former group. Either the innovators will draw the later adopters or alienate them. Many times, escaped slaves were drawn to free Black communities for assistance.

Before Harriet Tubman and Frederick Douglass, there was a free Black man named David Ruggles. Ruggles, who lived in New York, coordinated with William Still, a key figure on the Underground Railroad who kept thorough records of his work, in Philadelphia to help interstate slave escapes. Ruggles was born to free parents in Connecticut, where he was raised and educated. As Graham Russell Gao Hodges notes in *David Ruggles: A Radical Black Abolitionist and the Underground Railroad in New York City,* Ruggles understood what slavery was and despised the institution. When he was old enough to leave home, he settled in New York City, where he accomplished a great deal before he had turned 25. Ruggles helped organize the New York Committee of Vigilance in 1835, and he later helped then-slave Frederick Bailey, better known as Frederick Douglass, escape, as Ruggles' home was a stop on the Underground Railroad.

As previously mentioned, a key principle for some was to save their family members. Some slaves wouldn't try to escape without their loved ones. Enslaved men were known to do what they could to preserve, protect, and provide for their families. Talk, game, and radio show host Steve Harvey, in his best-seller-turned-movie *Act Like a Lady, Think Like a Man,* says that when a man wants a woman, he will profess, protect, and provide for her. Even in slavery, men honored this commitment. Sound principles can force innovation.

A man proposed marriage to a young woman named Lear Green, (some slaves married in spite of the laws against such unions) who had recently come into the hands of the Nobles family as part of an inheritance. Her new mistress was cruel, and Lear had to secure her freedom. Her creative method for escape was chronicled in William Still's *The Underground Railroad: Authentic Narratives and First-Hand Accounts.* The mother of the man she intended to marry was a free Black woman; the plan required her to be a passenger on a boat with Lear. The catch was Lear wasn't going to purchase a ticket; instead, a chest was used to conceal her body. It had minimal bedding in it, a little food and water, and was fastened tight to sail on the ship. After eighteen hours in the chest, Lear was a free woman in the hands of members of the Philadelphia Vigilance Committee. It was a courageous and innovative escape.

In addition to the abolitionists, some fell into the anti-slavery group. In social scientist Everett Rogers' discussion of innovation adoption, this group could be among the early adopters. They opposed the institution, but didn't agree with free Blacks living in their communities. In *Make Free,* William Breyfogle notes that many poor Whites helped fugitive slaves because the plantation system compromised their ability to secure employment. They didn't want the institution to persist, but they also didn't want to compete with Blacks, whether slave or free. Some Whites favored gradual emancipation as opposed to eradicating the system in its entirety; some in this group opposed the control the South attempted to impose on the North. As Southerners wanted their political control to extend beyond their natural boundaries, some Northerners joined the Free Soil political party.

In the late eighteenth century, America's first political parties were the Federalist and Democratic-Republican parties: the Federalists wanted the Federal government to control the economic growth of the nation (through national banks, for example), while the Democratic-Republican Party (also known as the Jeffersonian Republicans) favored states' rights over national government control. Ultimately, the Democrats dropped the Republicans during President Andrew Jackson's administration. Some of the Republicans wanted to abolish or limit slavery, while the Democrats wanted to preserve and expand it. The Whig Party formed in opposition to the Democratic Party. They believed in Congressional power but could not agree on the question of slavery, leading to the party's demise.

At the time, many Democrats supported slavery, states' rights, and Southern political power. There were some Democrats who didn't agree with the Slave Power, a minority of Southern landowners using the free labor of the enslaved; dissidents believed slavery compromised the independence of free White farmers. Thus, the Free Soil Party was formed from members who left the Democratic and Whig Parties. The Republican Party formed in the 1850s, consisting of Free Soilers, abolitionists, Northern Democrats and others.

According to Christopher J. Olsen in *The American Civil War*, members of the Free Soil Party didn't want slavery in the West; they didn't want working class families to compete with "wealthy slave owners for good land" and free labor depressing the wages for free Whites. They also didn't want slavery in their regions to promote the growth of the South's political power. Some Northerners supported the Free Soil Party because they felt slavery was wrong, but there were some in the early adopters category who were more likely to challenge the laws enforcing slavery than to aid a fugitive en route to freedom. Depending on the depth of their convictions and their principles, they may have helped fugitives along the Underground Railroad.

Some people were displeased with the dominant Democratic Party run by the Slave power. While some joined the Free Soil Party however others joined the Liberty Party, founded by philanthropist Gerrit Smith. According to Fergus Bordewich in *Bound for Canaan,* it was the first political Party in America to advocate the immediate abolition of slavery. The Party never won an election, yet it was a central way to organize activities to fight the Slave Power. However, according to Siebert, most abolitionists were members of the Whig Party.

The Whig party was made up mostly of Northerners with anti-slavery views, as opposed to the decidedly pro-slavery Democrats. The Republican Party did not embrace abolitionism like the Free Soilers did; they were anti-slavery for political and economic reasons. The combined vote of the Republican, Whig, Free Soil, and Liberty Parties, as well as the support of other dissidents, helped to elect Abraham Lincoln to the presidency in 1860.

Returning to Rogers' innovation adoption categories, another group consisted of those who did nothing for or against slavery. Rogers might say this group formed the early and late majority. Some didn't care or couldn't afford to get involved in the political debate about slavery or the efforts along the Underground Railroad; they were focused on their family's survival. Ironically, members of this group were the most likely to fight in the Civil War. Olsen discusses the laws protecting "wealthy, educated, and middle-class men" from being drafted into service, while men with money could hire others to serve in their place. This led some to complain it was "a rich man's war but a poor man's fight." These legal provisions caused disunity among Confederate supporters.

In terms of principles and commitment to freedom, slave catchers, those who would track down fugitive slaves for pay, could also fall into the Everett Rogers final category of innovation adoption: the laggards. They were typically less affluent, non-slaveholders attempting to improve their lot in life. Yet another reason fugitives and abolitionists had to be creative on a moment's notice: some slave catchers would help the abolitionists or the slave owners for money. In this sense, they were double agents. In *The Liberty Line,* Larry Gara discusses how some guides were paid to help fugitives, such as ship captains taking money to transport slaves or others being compensated for housing slaves. Gara argues they were not part of the Underground Railroad because they couldn't be trusted; their principles were not sound. In spite of the dangers, there were some Whites who helped fugitives along the way.

Levi Coffin was an abolitionist and an innovator committed to freeing the enslaved. In the foreword of the abridged and edited version of *Reminiscences* by Ben Richmond, Coffin said, "I had not desire to appear before the public as an author, having no claim to literary merit. What I had done I believed was simply a Christian duty and not for the purpose of being seen of men, or for notoriety, which I have never sought. But I was continually urged by my friends to engage in the work..." What a powerful sentiment! Doing right for the sake of doing right. Coffin supported the fugitives based on the biblical principle man should be free. His principles caused some slave owners to put a bounty on his life. Yet he remained committed: "As to my safety, my life was in the hands of the Divine Master, and I felt that I had his approval. I had no fear of the danger that seemed to threaten my life or my business."

Fugitives knew Coffin was a friend on the Underground Railroad. In his memoirs, he described two Negro boys showing up at his home. When a U.S. marshall questioned Coffin about their whereabouts, Coffin said, "I saw two such boys, not half an hour since, pass this gate; they inquired where the Cincinnati, Hamilton and Dayton depot was, and if you haste you may reach the depot before the train leaves." Coffin didn't say whether the boys went in or out of his gate; they had been in his home the entire time. "Runaway slaves used frequently to conceal themselves in the woods and thickets in the vicinity of New Garden, waiting opportunities to make their escape to the North, and I generally learned their places of concealment and rendered them all the service in my power." In Coffin's mind, the deception was not a lie; he was standing on the principle of freedom.

Author Fergus Bordewich describes how Coffin also helped create a new language while working on the UGRR. "When Levi Coffin told the men from Union County to 'switch off your locomotives,' and 'let them blow off steam,' remarking that seventeen passengers were as many as 'the cars' could bear at one time, he was using a brand new language that, to Americans of the 1840s, was as fresh as the language of the Internet was to wired Americans at the end of the twentieth century." Creating a new language or vocabulary is a trademark of innovation. In *Mavericks at Work*, Taylor and LaBarre note when companies are truly trying something new, they may create a "strategic vocabulary." This isn't a joke; it's a decisive way to distinguish culture and commitment. It is a mark of originality and lets those involved know the principles to be valued.

Ironically, the new language online often has a historic connection. For example, links are akin to routes, while portals can be likened to safe houses, barns, and other hiding places. Revisiting the concepts of branding and tagging, "branding" is a controversial word with regards to slavery; in contemporary society, it refers to leaving an indelible mark in one's mind, while in slavery, it referred to the indelible marks made in a slave's flesh by their overseers. Just like the brands on the backs of the slave, brands, tags, and information in the twenty-first century are public and permanent. When discussing Internet safety and creating your reputation in the virtual world, I often tell groups, "online your sins may be forgiven, but they will not be forgotten." As facial recognition improves, you may have an alias, but your face will still be identifiable. In addition, your digital footprint will last after your flesh returns to the dust. Think strategically about your language, brand, and lasting legacy.

Remaining on track, another conductor on the road to freedom was Dr. Isaac Beck from Sardinia, Ohio. In a letter to Wilbur Siebert, Dr. Beck wrote, "We operated differently from the railroads, our aim was safety not speed, for it made little difference to the fugitive whether he was a week or a month in getting to Canada, so that he got there safely and was fed on his way". They understood that innovation takes time. This is a valuable lesson: the end goal is more important than the means. Dr. Beck and others wanted to make sure their passengers safely arrived at their destination. Many who aided the fugitives had convictions so strong they passed them down to future generations, expanding and strengthening the effectiveness of the UGRR.

The Reverend John Rankin, an abolitionist and minister from Ripley, Ohio, worked with his wife and children to secure safety for escaped slaves. In *Beyond the River*, Ann Hagedorn relates the story of Theodore and Thomas Collins, also lived of Ripley, Ohio, continuing their father's legacy on the UGRR. To avoid raising suspicion, the brothers would hide fugitive slaves in coffins. This innovative technique is often attributed to Levi Coffin (for obvious reasons). Dr. William Taft supported his father's efforts as well, saying in an interview for *The Commercial Tribune* that "…this was the strongest rivets in the framework of the underground system, teaching the value of sympathy and silence to children."

Another story was related by William Breyfogle. John Hume's father would hide slaves in an old barn on their property, and also transported fugitives from one safe house to the next. On one particular day, neither John's father nor his brother was available. The younger Hume hitched up his father's horses to a tailored wagon to drive his passengers to the next station. "In the bed of the wagon, under an old buffalo robe that was to shelter the travelers from the weather, his mother put a smoke-cured ham wrapped in loose rags. Apparently, this was a standard precaution on that particular route. The purpose was to kill any possible smell of Negroes that might persist in the wagon." The on-the-spot creativity was beyond amazing. Nobody had time to judge whether it would work or not, they just did what was necessary. The younger Hume supported his father's principles and used innovative means to reach the desired end.

In addition to the children of abolitionists, some of the sons of slaveholders helped some fugitives. It was common for young slaves to be raised with the children of the master of the plantation; children play with each other until they are taught not to do so, and relationships naturally developed. The messages can be implicit or explicit from television, teachers, preachers, parents, or peers. This was clear in my dissertation research *The Role of Race in Black Student Intragroup Peer Interactions: A Qualitative Analysis.* External factors seemingly have the greatest impact on peer relationships. As the children of slaveholders watched the abuse slaves endured, some hearts were softened. At a certain age, their best friends became their property.

Robert Purvis helped to organize the National Negro Convention. In 1838, he was in charge of the Philadelphia Vigilance Committee. Like William Still, Purvis kept records about the UGRR activities. In *Let My People Go,* Henrietta Buckmaster shared Purvis' account about the son of slaveholders. "Another most efficient worker was a son of a slaveholder who lived at Newberne, North Carolina. Through his agency the slaves were forwarded by placing them on vessels engaged in the lumber trade which plied between Newberne and Philadelphia, and the captains of which had heart." Yet another strategic and innovative way to transport human "cargo." Hearts filled with courage and compassion facilitated the escapes. They stood on the principles passed down to them from their parents.

The Underground Railroad had to operate in silence and secrecy. Although Purvis and a few others like Coffin and Still kept records, most of the information had to be destroyed in order to protect the UGRR. This presented a real dilemma for historians, but thanks to Wilbur Siebert, there is substantial proof the UGRR existed. Those who participated didn't do it for the recognition; they preferred keeping their activities private. Although one of the principles online is transparency, the ways some fugitives were helped to escape could not be broadcast. It was somewhat ironic: the Underground operated in plain view, yet was invisible. This same principle and conviction from the Underground Railroad is evident in cyberspace today.

The Internet is supposed to be a free space, unowned by anyone. However, through copyright and other legal actions, some companies are attempting to control what some refer to as the "virtual Wild West." Professor Yochai Benkler cites the work of James Boyle when he quotes, "The freedom of action for individuals who wish to produce information, knowledge, and culture is being systematically curtailed in order to secure the economic returns demanded by the manufacturers of the industrial information economy." Money is always a factor. The slave owners in the South were furious when slaves were allowed refuge in northern cities, feeling betrayed by the "thieving Yankees." It is peculiar how the Southerners called the Northerners thieves considering that Southerners imported humans from Africa, turning them into inanimate objects. Hypocrisy runs deep.

Good innovation is rooted in principle, not principal. When a project grows on a solid foundation, it flourishes in unimaginable ways. Money follows sound principles; when money is the means to an end, efforts may go awry. What is the value and worth of the innovation? If it can only be described in monetary terms, it may not prosper. Those who chase money will seldom catch it, and if they do, they may not be able to keep it. Those who stand on principles are rich with or without compensation. The love the slave owners had for money, power, and greed forced many enslaved Africans to seek freedom along the Underground Railroad, and it was the principle of freedom that sustained one of the most effective, innovative, and disruptive networks in American history.

SUMMARY

- Like the Internet, the Underground Railroad was a peer-to-peer network.

- The Internet and UGRR leveraged extra capacity through strangers working together to realize the end goal of freedom and access.

- Josiah Henson is the enslaved African many believe was fictionalized in Harriet Beecher Stowe's book *Uncle Tom's Cabin*.

- Henson was a faithful slave turned fugitive, rescuing his family and ultimately starting a school in Canada.

- Some Blacks were free in America: some were born free, others purchased their freedom by paying off their debt, and some owners emancipated their slaves.

- The enslaved and their UGRR supporters went to great lengths to promote, preserve, and protect the principle of freedom.

- The political parties proliferated partially in response to beliefs about slavery, freedom, and political power.

- The Democratic-Republican Party split into the Democrat and Republican Parties. At the time, the Democratic Party was pro-slavery, while other, anti-slavery parties formed, such as the Free Soil Party, the Liberty Party, and the Whig Party.

- Northerners opposed slavery to varying degrees. Some wanted it abolished, some wanted it limited to the South, some wanted the enslaved Africans freed and returned to Africa, and some didn't have a problem with slavery.

- Levi Coffin, a prominent conductor on the UGRR, believed in the biblical and constitutional principle that all men were created equal.

- The ability to create a new language can be a sign of innovation. On the UGRR, coded messages were as critical as passwords are on the Internet.

- The UGRR routes are akin to today's websites and portals on the Internet.

CHAPTER SEVEN

Purpose

"Success demands singleness of purpose."

VINCE LOMBARDI

Innovation has a purpose. How will the innovation be used? Where will implementation of the new idea lead? How does it affect the current state of the industry? And if the innovation is disruptive, what new audience will it reveal? The purpose of the Underground Railroad was to provide support for fugitive slaves. The conductors were determined to facilitate a slave's successful quest for freedom. It was their job to send the fugitives in the right direction, but they didn't have established goals to save a certain number of escapees. They didn't have Google analytics or other measures to quantify their progress; success was their only goal. Proving an escape would work in advance was impossible, and they couldn't keep track of how many were saved. Most UGRR conductors wouldn't document the escapes for fear of legal prosecution, though there were some who dared to record their experiences.

As a child, Levi Coffin watched the indignities of slavery while growing up in North Carolina. One day, Coffin was chopping wood with his father when they saw a chain gang, a group of slaves chained together. In *Reminiscences of Levi Coffin* edited by Ben Richmond, Coffin said the men's posture and appearance did not represent their intelligence. In Africa, some were leaders, inventors, and educators. Coffin realized the men were much greater than their current circumstance. Coffin's father asked the men why they were chained; the response was to prevent escape. After all, the men had been separated from their families and would do anything to see their wives and children. This left an indelible mark on young Levi and awakened his deeper purpose.

Levi Coffin was a Quaker, and many in this faith believed God made all men to be free. Quakers were also known as "The Society of Friends." Some set up schools for the enslaved, fugitives, and free Blacks. Others supported the cause with more tangible resources, such as money, shelter, and food. In the Methodist Church, a group of abolitionists left the main church to form the Wesleyan Methodists, a group supporting the enslaved. Presbyterians, some Indians, immigrants, and other settlers also helped those on the run to escape. Although some did, most abolitionists did not entice enslaved Africans to leave. Recall that as a matter of principle, most felt it wasn't right to go to the plantations to get the enslaved; they instead aided runaways as the scripture instructed them to do: feeding the hungry and clothing the naked.

As an adult, Coffin moved his family from North Carolina to Richmond, Indiana, where the majority of his service on the Underground Railroad took place. He was a successful businessman with resources through the banking and mill industries. His home quickly became known as a safe haven on the UGRR; given his location, there was no shortage of passengers. Coffin's bravery encouraged others to get involved. People watched Coffin helping strangers and many decided to help too. When people take a chance, others may follow.

Levi's cousin, Addison Coffin, was also an UGRR conductor. Addison explained how serving a God-given purpose could take its toll, saying conductors could only serve for about ten years before the mental, emotional, and physical fatigue became too much to bear. This is a critical point. Innovation can be exhausting. Fighting for an idea to be heard and/or tried can take its toll. Pulling all-nighters to realize the vision demands the need for rest. Addison was close to having a nervous breakdown when he left North Carolina to live in Indiana near his cousin Levi. Addison's brother was run out of North Carolina when he was exposed as a friend of the enslaved, but the risks were worth it to these men. In spite of the dangers they faced, many ministers used their pulpits, position and prayers to help end the South's peculiar institution.

John Rankin was a Presbyterian minister from Ripley, Ohio, who believed in abolition. He wasn't alone: his wife and their thirteen children also aided fugitives fleeing enslavement. Their home, which still stands today, overlooks the Ohio River and became a safe haven for hundreds of runaways. In some his personal writings housed at the Union Township Public Library in Ripley, Rankin shared this account: "Another young slave woman came from Maysville to my house. She was beautiful and accomplished in her manners and but slightly colored. She was a seamstress and, as such had intercourse with the highest class of ladies, from whom she gained knowledge and learned politeness. She would have been glad to make her home with my family but that could not be done. The slave catchers would soon have found her and taken her back to slavery. Several other fugitive slaves were with her including the man who wanted to marry her once they made it to Canada. On the Underground Railway they were conducted to the land of freedom." Rankin felt it was his purpose to help people in bondage.

Author Fergus Bordewich called Rankin a "moral entrepreneur". This is the equivalent of today's social entrepreneur. This involves leveraging and building positive social capital for social good. Creating partnerships and having a presence and a purpose are also imperative in the digital age. In *Digital Leader: 5 Simple Keys to Success and Influence*, author Erik Qualman gives his STAMP for virtual wins in leadership. The acronym stands for simplicity, truth, action, mapping, and people. All were present on the Underground Railroad. The simplest routes were often the safest; complicated plans could lead to tragic endings. Truth was often manipulated to realize the desired end, safe passage for a passenger; yet, the end goal was absolute freedom. Truth was freedom. Making decisive choices was critical, and could easily determine whether one failed or succeeded; indecision could sometimes be worse than making the wrong decision.

Mapping involved having a vision and moving toward it. Many enslaved Africans heard about the "promised land" of Canada, but few knew where it was or how long it would take to get there. By faith, they set off on their journeys, embracing the unknown and making history along the way. Finally, the UGRR was a man-made network created and sustained by people. Qualman says to "network before you need your network." For enslaved Africans, this was possible at times. Having people in the right place when you needed them most was literally life saving.

John Rankin was in position to realize his purpose. He accepted his call to preach, serve, and befriend the friendless. He was even in the right location to fulfill his purpose. Researcher Fergus Bordewich provides three major reasons why Ripley, Ohio was an ideal place for service on the Underground. There were a number of Presbyterian ministers settling in Ripley, who were leaving the South to avoid slavery. Their ability to politicize the issue through the creation and organization of anti-slavery societies was another reason. In addition, many free Blacks lived near the Ohio River, strategically located to help fugitives seeking refuge in the North via Kentucky. Nature forced the enslaved to adapt and to innovate according to their circumstance. Sadly, the full extent of their innovative abilities will never be known.

As previously mentioned, UGRR participants could not document their efforts, but newspaper editors and reporters could. The newspaper was America's first mass medium, reigning unchallenged until the rise of radio more than two hundred years later. Many newspapers ran pro-slavery stories yielding to the power, position, and politics of slave owners; in most accounts, the enslaved were portrayed as the aggressors. This is well-documented in the Juan Gonzalez and Joseph Torres bestseller *News for All People: The Epic Story of Race and the American Media*. Pro-slavery newspapers were delivered without interruption, while news supporting the enslaved or chronicling pro-abolitionist activity was often not mailed at the Postmaster's discretion. This forced yet another disruption.

John Russwurm and Samuel Cornish published the first Negro paper in the United States in 1827. *Freedom's Journal* gave abolitionists, the enslaved, and free Blacks a public platform to present their case against the legalized institution. The newspapers and pamphlets were often carried into the Southern states by White abolitionists and supporters of the anti-slavery movement. It was an extremely dangerous mission; some were jailed or even killed for their efforts. The Black press was an essential part of the freedom movement, allowing the voiceless to be heard.

In *Beyond the River*, author Ann Hagedorn mentions a Quaker named Elihu Embree who created the nation's "first periodical to focus exclusively on the cause of ending slavery." Originally called the *Manumission Intelligencer*, the name was later changed to *The Emancipator*. In 1815, Benjamin Lundy created *The Genius of Universal Emancipation*, determined to "spread the news of freedom." Henrietta Buckmaster chronicled Lundy's effort to publish the truth: "The only available press was at Mount Pleasant, Ohio, twenty miles from his home and he walked between the two towns, his edition on his back." Excuses were irrelevant. When people had a purpose, they pursued it.

In 1831, William Lloyd Garrison published *The Liberator*. Garrison, a poor boy from Massachusetts, was raised by his mother once his father left the family when Garrison was three. Early on he worked with shoe- and cabinet-makers, but he found his calling at age 13 when he did a printing apprenticeship. He hated slavery and wanted it abolished immediately. After founding his abolitionist newspaper in Boston, he was accused of libel, printing false statements regarding slavery and jailed as a result. Judicial officials decided if the information was factual; unfortunately, some were pro-slavery. Garrison's words in the first issue of *The Liberator* clearly asserted his "non-conformist" position on slavery:

> "I will be as harsh as truth, and as uncompromising as justice. On this subject, I do not wish to think, or speak, or write, with moderation. No! no! Tell a man whose house is on fire, to give moderate alarm; tell him to moderately rescue his wife from the hand of the ravisher; tell the mother to gradually extricate her babe from the fire into which it has fallen; — but urge me not to use moderation in a cause like the present. I am earnest— I will not equivocate—I will not excuse—I will not retreat a single inch— AND I WILL BE HEARD. The apathy of the people is enough to make every statue leap from its pedestal, and to hasten the resurrection of the dead." – William Lloyd Garrison, *The Liberator*.

Garrison did not waiver. He was an innovative risk taker, going on to help establish the American Anti-Slavery Society. As an interesting historical side note, Maria Stewart, who is believed to be the first black

female journalist, wrote for *The Liberator*. Garrison also inspired abolitionist Frederick Douglass. After hearing Garrison speak at an anti-slavery
meeting and being invited to speak himself, Garrison encouraged the former slave, who soon began his own career in public speaking, even starting
his own newspaper, *The North Star*, in 1847. In it he denounced racism
and sexism. From any platform, he stood up for all oppressed people. Douglass leveraged his access to people whether in person or from afar.

This is the same concept author Jeff Jarvis shares in *What Would Google
Do?* Jarvis talks about creating a platform where others can participate, giving and receiving value, with Facebook being a prime example of an online
community square. *The North Star* was circulated to more than 4,000 readers in the United States. Douglass also helped fugitives on the Underground Railroad, although he didn't agree with publicizing the activities
of the network, calling it the "upper-ground" railroad because of some
detailed newspaper accounts. Still, Black publishers were determined to
spread the stories of the enslaved.

Henry Bibb was another such publisher, starting Canada's first black
newspaper, *Voice of the Fugitive*, in 1851. Like Frederick Douglass and
countless other slaves, Bibb had a Black mother and a White father, and
like many enslaved Africans, Bibb was motivated to escape because the
woman he loved bore his child. He made it to freedom several times, but
was caught and returned to slavery when he would go back to get his family. Author Fergus Bordewich shared Bibbs' story: "After an attempted
escape with his wife and daughter, Bibb was stripped, staked spreadeagle
on the ground, and savagely flogged, first with a bull whip, and then with
a flat wooden paddle. For weeks afterward, he was also made to wear heavy
iron collar with prongs extending above his head, on the end of which dan-
gled a small, humiliating bell." These accounts are deliberately shared, lest
the horrors of slavery be forgotten.

Bibb finally secured his freedom, but his beloved Malinda had given
up on him. He eventually settled in Detroit but moved to Canada after
the Fugitive Slave Act of 1850 was passed. As a journalist, he interviewed
former slaves who made it to freedom. In his first issue of the *Voice of the
Fugitive*, Bibb defined the paper's purpose: "We need a press, that we may
be independent of those who have always oppressed us. We need a press

that we may hang our banners on the wall, that all who pass by may read why we struggle, and what we struggle for." According to the late historian John Hope Franklin, other papers included *The Mystery* (Pittsburgh, 1843), *The Colored Man's Journal* (New York, 1851), *The Mirror of Times* (San Francisco, 1855), and *The Anglo-African* (New York, 1859).

Slaveholders were often well aware of the activities of abolitionists and newspaper publishers, and some Southern editors lost their lives for expressing unpopular opinions. In 1837, one of the first White martyrs during the UGRR movement was Elijah P. Lovejoy, a Presbyterian minister originally from Maine who became a newspaper publisher in Alton, Illinois. Lovejoy was attacked several times, and later became the editor of *The Observer*, a newspaper in St. Louis. Initially, he was in favor of gradual emancipation, but when he embraced immediate emancipation, things turned deadly; an angry mob shot him to death for his anti-slavery views. Thousands joined the abolitionists following Lovejoy's murder. Lawyer and philanthropist Wendell Phillips was inspired by Lovejoy's death: "How prudently most men creep into nameless graves while now and then one or two forget themselves into the immortality."

Newspapers also served the purpose of slave owners, advertising runaway slaves. Here is a sample call from historian John Hope Franklin for the return of property:

> "Absconded from the Forest Plantation of the late William Dunbar, on Sunday the 7th instant, a very handsome Mulattress (black and white mixed racial heritage) called Harriet, about 13 years old, with straight dark hair and dark eyes. This girl was lately in New Orleans, and is known to have seen there a man whom she claims as her father and who does now or did lately live on the Mississippi, a little above the mouth of the Caffalaya. It is highly probable some plan has been concerted for the girl's escape…"

Classified ads generated substantial income for newspapers until Craig Newmark created the online classified service Craigslist, allowing people to bypass physical newspapers and to reach a global audience with their placed ads. The UGRR helped fugitives bypass detection and provided greater access to freedom across the border in Canada.

Another purpose-driven abolitionist was Salmon P. Chase, a lawyer from Cincinnati, Ohio. Chase served as a Senator and Governor in Ohio, later becoming the Secretary of the Treasury and then serving as the 6th Chief Justice of the Supreme Court. He vigorously fought the Slave Power, those who wanted to control the rest of the country. He created several legal briefs, including the foundation of the Free Soil Party and coined the party slogan of "Free Soil, Free Labor, Free Men," a position later embraced by the new Republican Party. The Chase National Bank was named after him; now known as the JPMorgan Chase Bank, their "freedom" advertising campaign is an acknowledgment of this connection. Chase Bank was a key supporter in helping to build the National Underground Railroad Freedom Center in Cincinnati, Ohio.

Abolitionists tended to be from the middle and upper classes and well educated, which allowed them to have greater access to the media. They could afford to subscribe to newspapers during a time when the masses could not afford the luxury. This is in line with the elite, popular, and specialized (E-P-S) Mass Media model developed by scholars John Merrill and Ralph Lowenstein. An individual consumes a medium, for example television, movies, or radio, because they can afford the initial higher price for the new technology. Once the price drops, the medium's exposure is greatly broadened. Finally, once it is in the mass population, it then specializes; magazines are a prime example of this model's development.

In 1830, newspaper publisher Benjamin Day started the penny press, dropping the price for a newspaper by five cents. It was a now-classic revenue move: drop the price, increase access and overall consumption, then make more money. Traditional companies are less likely to employ this strategy, whereas emerging companies have the freedom to experiment and take greater risks. Day's papers favored advertising over subscriptions, and used newsboys standing on corners to sell papers for a wider distribution channel. Compulsory public education in 1840 lead to more people learning how to read; all these factors combined to create an ideal mass audience for newspapers.

The middle and upper classes were the most influential voters and political participants. Understanding their audience, a few newspaper editors made sure to promote the purpose of the Underground Railroad and the anti-slavery movement. They wanted the elite to be aware of the atrocities of slavery. Those with money had more opportunities to read information from various sources. When Harriett Beecher Stowe published *Uncle Tom's Cabin* in 1852, she had no idea it would become a best seller, ultimately playing a critical role in changing many hearts and minds about slavery. In *The American Civil War*, Christopher J. Olsen remarked that "The book presents slavery as a life of cruelty and tragedy, and emphasizes how it destroyed the character of Southern whites and undermined all families, slave and free, by allowing white men—portrayed often in the book as violent, drunk, sadistic rapists—to act with impunity." The story was reprinted in newspapers, performed in theaters, and even used in public schools. Using books, newspapers, pamphlets, and newsletters to promote the cause of freedom was an important strategy for supporting the UGRR and the abolition of slavery.

Slaves were prohibited by law from learning how to read, but that did little to dissuade them; some learned how to read from their owners or from their owners' children. Frederick Douglass was taught how to read by his owner's wife. She knew it was against the law to teach a slave how to read, and her husband reminded her of the violation as soon as he learned what she had done. In his autobiography Douglass said, "A [slave] should know nothing but to obey his master—to do as he is told to do. Learning would spoil the best [slave] in the world. ...if you teach that (Frederick) [slave] how to read, there would be no keeping him. It would forever unfit him to be a slave." In that moment, Frederick made up his mind to learn how to read. The free or enslaved Blacks understood the power of an education. They read in the dark, behind barns, in the shadows, and wherever they could to improve their lots in life. Education was not taken for granted.

Many slaves knew education was a critical factor for their emancipation, but in twenty-first century America, some no longer value education; it is so readily accessible, and from a psychological perspective, people want things most when they are perceived to be scarce. It's a foundational principle in marketing. Author Chris Anderson put it this way in his book *Free:* "If we get what we're seeking, we tend to quickly discount it and find a new scarcity to pursue. We are motivated by what we do not have, not what we do have." During slavery, freedom was scarce and a group of free and enslaved people waged a fierce battle to obtain it. It's a stark contrast, yet such an important reminder to value what really is valuable. Education is priceless. In the networked economy, intellectual capital is worth gold.

In *The World is Flat,* journalist Thomas Friedman said, "The members of the first generation are nose to the grindstone innovators; the second generation holds it together; then their kids come along and get fat, dumb, and lazy and slowly squander it all." Ironically, this loosely fits into the innovation adoption categories, with the second generation in the early adopter and early and late majority categories and the third generation consisting of laggards. Clayton Christensen, Michael B. Horn, and Curtis W. Johnson posit the same in *Disrupting Class: How Disruptive Innovation Will Change the Way the World Learns.* These authors believe American children lack motivation in the land of plenty. They are not deprived of food or other essential resources; therefore, they take a lot for granted. This explains the experiences of the third generation Friedman says squanders opportunities.

In *The Age of Access,* economist Jeremy Rifkin said, "Intellectual capital, on the other hand, is the driving force of the new era, and much coveted. Concepts, ideas and image—not things—are the real items of value in the new economy." Therefore, schools are needed, just not in their current con-figurations. During a TED talk, Sir Ken Robinson stresses the need to change the public education system still based on the factory model. This change isn't optional, and money cannot matter when the future is at stake. Principle has to take precedence over principal, and purpose must lead to the goal that will uphold humanity. It will be a costly overhaul, both men-tally and fiscally, yet absolutely necessary.

In the Internet age, distance learning, online learning, pop-up schools, and various other programs have emerged to capitalize on the virtual learning trend. Educators and administrators must innovate, not just copy limited examples of success. As Christensen and Eyring discuss in *The Innovative University,* copying is not creative. There is only one original institution of higher education in America, and that's Harvard. It is the model. "Harvard succeeded in becoming Harvard in large part because it never tried to become anything else." All others are copies. Copies fade. In

Out of Our Minds, Sir Ken Robinson said, "In the 21ˢᵗ century humanity faces some of its most daunting challenges. Our best resource is to cultivate our singular abilities of imagination, creativity and innovation." And that's where Rifkin believes the money is. "Wealth is no longer vested in physical capital but rather in human imagination and creativity."

Innovating by choice isn't always easy. The enslaved Africans and their "friends" were forced to engage in lateral thinking. They knew for every question, there were answers in the process, not just in solving the problem. They had to think differently. Their perspective facilitated, encouraged, and embraced creativity and innovation. It's a choice to be a disrupter or get disrupted. The Underground Railroad was an offensive strategy. It was an effective and innovative network, forcing people to shift their perspectives to survive and ultimately to succeed.

SUMMARY

- On the Underground Railroad, goals could not be projected or measured.
- Effectiveness was measured by successful escapes, yet most escapes could not be documented for fear the UGRR would be exposed.
- Abolitionist Levi Coffin used his position as a businessman to fulfill his purpose as a conductor on the UGRR.
- Rest and rejuvenation were necessary for conductors and agents on the UGRR.
- Residents of Ripley, Ohio were uniquely positioned to help fugitives on the UGRR.
- Then, UGRR supporters were called moral entrepreneurs. Today, they would be known as social entrepreneurs.
- Networking on the Underground Railroad was imperative. The same ability to connect with people is paramount on the Internet.
- Some newspaper editors and publishers played an integral role on the UGRR risking their lives to tell and to spread the stories about enslaved Africans and the peculiar institution.
- The Black press formed to create a platform challenging the injustices enforced by the Slave Power.
- The ability to read and to access newspapers, books, and other literature about the horrendous condition of enslaved Africans helped sway public opinion about slavery.

CHAPTER EIGHT

Perspective

"He that is willing to be a slave, let him be a slave."

HARRIET JACOBS

For the enslaved, their outlooks or perspectives were critical. Those who had a vision, a hope, or even a wish for a better life were more likely to attempt to escape and possibly travel through the Underground Railroad. Slave owners really couldn't prove the UGRR existed, and their perspective was that the system wasn't strong and couldn't end slavery. Arrogance often clouded their ability to see what was happening, and denial did not make the problem disappear. This attitude, combined with the battles over states' rights and the political power struggle to expand the slave system beyond just the southern states, ended in war.

To discuss the Underground Railroad without mentioning the Civil War would be shortsighted. In *Make Free,* William Breyfogle writes, "The Underground led into the Civil War; the Civil War completed the work the Underground had long been doing. Each was a part of a greater whole, and it would be arbitrary to try to divide one from the other." Historians record many reasons for the bloodiest and deadliest conflict in American history, such as political power, boundaries, greed, slavery, and freedom.

From the North to the South, from the original thirteen colonies in the East to the newest territories in the West, the very fabric of American society was at risk of being shredded beyond repair.

Initially, seven states separated from the Union: South Carolina, Texas, Florida, Alabama, Mississippi, Georgia, and Louisiana. In *Lies My Teacher Told Me Everything Your American History Textbook Got Wrong*, James W. Loewen cites slavery as the primary reason for the war. Lawmakers in South Carolina were furious some Northern states were not enforcing the Fugitive Slave Act. Loewen wrote, "Thus South Carolina opposed states' rights when claimed by free states. This is understandable. Historically, whatever faction has been out of power in America has pushed for states' rights." "States' rights" was sometimes used as a euphemism for segregation. Until 1860, White Southern Democrats held the most powerful positions in Congress. Loewen states, "Only after they lost control of the executive branch in the 1860 election did slave owners (Democrats) begin to suggest limiting federal power."

When the Civil War began at Fort Sumter in South Carolina and President Abraham Lincoln ordered Union troops to respond, four additional states joined the Confederacy: Arkansas, Tennessee, North Carolina, and Virginia. Enslaved Africans quickly turned the chaos into an opportunity for escape. This was a strategy they employed very well; author Christopher J. Olsen said, "Slaves had always taken advantage of confusion or division within the white community—tens of thousands ran away during the American Revolution and the War of 1812."

Most of the research of the events leading to the Civil War confirms the Southern mindset favored the past, while the Northern perspective was more future-oriented. William Breyfogle states the obvious in *Make Free*: "The South had already paid heavily—in adopting and then stubbornly adhering to a lopsided system that inhibited industrial and urban development, that went far toward destroying the fertility of Southern soil, and barely tolerated the existence of a white yeomanry." Attitudes are often the same toward innovation. One's perspective can be like concrete, gradually hardening and becoming impenetrable. Perspective also played a critical role in the conflict. Breyfogle says, "However gropingly, the North was moving toward a national outlook: the South remained stubbornly regional in its thinking. More than that, the South gave its allegiance to the past, while the North looked toward the future. At Fort Sumter the past and the future met."

People hang on to their past understandings, blinding themselves to present needs and future opportunities. In his research on disruptive innovation, Clayton Christensen writes, "Within a value network, each firm's competitive strategy, and particularly its past choices of markets, determines its perceptions of the economic value of a new technology." This is a dangerous practice in the fast-paced digital age. The "value network" includes the current competitors with little if any regard for new entrants.

According to historian Wilbur Siebert, "It is safe to say that the Underground Railroad was one of the greatest forces which brought on the Civil War, and thus destroyed slavery." This powerful, principle-based network holds a myriad of lessons for any generation. It was organic by nature, grounded in the principles of freedom and honor, formed outside of the existing system, spread virally, and maximized the peer-to-peer network. It was especially effective in certain regions because it was a local network operating on the free and slave state boundaries.

In *Border War: Fighting Over Slavery Before the Civil War*, author Stanley Harrold contends the geographic boundaries between the North and the South led to the Civil War. "Instead, the proximity of the Lower North (Illinois, Indiana, Ohio, Iowa & Pennsylvania) and Border South (Virginia, Kentucky & Missouri), combined with the regions divergent economies, cultures, moralities, and—especially—their opposing views of slavery, led to physical clashes and expectations they would spread. Improved transportation, weak state authority, a law enforcement system dependent on private initiative, and a code of masculine honor encouraged the clashes." Having free and slave states so close together provided the enslaved with access to freedom and because of the Underground Railroad, thousands made it to the Promised Land.

At the beginning of the twenty-first century in America, perspective is the primary reason some remain entrenched in the industrial, factory age mindset, while others are embracing the digital, knowledge age mindset. Change is difficult for many. In *The Prince*, Machiavelli wrote, "I believe also that he will be successful who directs his actions according to the spirit of the times, and that he whose actions do not accord with the times will not be successful." This quote is from an edited version of *The Prince* written by Marc A. Moore:

> "But a man is not often found sufficiently circumspect to know how to accommodate himself to the change, both because he cannot deviate from what nature inclines him to do and also because, having always prospered by acting in one way, he cannot be persuaded that it is well to leave it; and, therefore, the cautious man, when it is time to turn adventurous, does not know how to do it, hence he is ruined; but had he changed his conduct with the times, fortune would not have changed."

Changing gears, politically speaking, Congressional leaders had been entangled in a verbal civil war for years. John Quincy Adams was a member of the U.S. House of Representatives. The son of America's second president, John Adams, the younger Adams argued vehemently to preserve the Constitution. He didn't necessarily oppose slavery, but he believed all people should have the right to petition the government according the Constitution. This position made Adams an anti-slavery man. This was a crucial issue leading up to the War.

Northerners didn't want their personal liberty laws or states' rights to be dictated by the Southern minority. Christopher J. Olsen shared this quote President Abraham Lincoln's first inaugural address: "The rule of a minority, as a permanent arrangement, is wholly inadmissible; so that, rejecting the majority principle, anarchy or despotism in some form is all that is left..."

Leading up to the Battle of Gettysburg, Abraham Lincoln emancipated the slaves. When the President signed the Emancipation Proclamation in 1863, it only freed the enslaved in the seceded Confederate states; slavery was still technically legal in the Union until the 13th Amendment abolished slavery in the United States in 1865. In the end, free enslaved Africans gave the Union some much-needed manpower, and further weakened the Confederacy.

To some, this gesture is seen as his support of the enslaved because it changed the nature of the war; however, Olsen notes that President Lincoln fought to preserve the Union, not to free the slave. "President Lincoln tried to keep slavery out of any discussion of the war, repeating that he was fighting only to restore the Union and uphold the principles of popular government and majority rule." Author and educator James Loewen contends most people don't read the entire Gettysburg Address or the entire texts of Lincoln's speeches. He points out that President Lincoln was a master politician, and he was keenly aware that slavery was too volatile an issue to present in clear terms; instead, the President emphasized freedom for all in his speeches. Here's an excerpt from Lincoln's second Inaugural Address:

> "Fondly do we hope—fervently do we pray—that this mighty scourge of war may speedily pass away. Yet, if God wills that it continue until all the wealth piled by the bondman's two hundred and fifty years of unrequited toil shall be sunk, and until every drop of blood drawn with the lash shall be paid by another drawn with the sword, as we said three thousand years ago, so still it must be said, 'The judgments of the Lord are true and righteous altogether'."

In the movie *Lincoln*, director Steven Spielberg captures the complexities of the 16th President's situation. Focusing on Mr. Lincoln's efforts to get the House of Representatives to pass the 13th Amendment to the Constitution, the unwavering commitment of then chairman of the House, Ways and Means Committee Thaddeus Stevens was also depicted; Stevens was a conductor on the UGRR in Pennsylvania and represented fugitives in court. Ultimately, the 13th Amendment passed in January 1865, and the President was assassinated in April of the same year.

To understand the Civil War, many historians advise students to take a closer look at the Battle of Gettysburg. As a participant in the American Press Institute Leadership in Disruptive Times seminar, retired U.S. Colonel Tom Vossler, former Director of the U.S. Army Military History Institute, provided great insight about the battle. Col. Vossler explained a battlefield normally has measurable dimensions, and the terrain has a big impact on the outcome. The Battle of Gettysburg began at McPherson's Ridge. Some wooded areas were smaller then due to the use of trees for lumber and constructing buildings. Eleven roads provided access to the battlefield at Gettysburg, facilitating movement of large armies. The location was ideal.

Col. Vossler noted for the most part, Confederate armies were named after geographic locations, while the Union armies were named for tributaries. The symbolism here cannot be ignored. Water flows, while geography is all about immovable boundaries and control. Nature teaches a great deal about life, death and perspective—thoughts worth pondering (TWP). Today, some traditional companies would be named after geographic locations while new entrant companies would be named after tributaries.

Like the waters that flow, the UGRR was fluid. It appeared and disappeared at will. New people, whether conductors or fugitives, participated freely in the decentralized network. They were not locked into a plan or a mindset; their only goal was to help people make it to safety. This is how so many organic movements are being facilitated online.

The days leading up to the pivotal battle on July 3, 1863 were filled with strategy. Union officer John Buford coordinated with General John F. Reynolds, sending him information about the terrain. This is a key lesson: assess the situation, observing not just what you want to see, but what you need to see. Centuries later, U.S. Air Force Colonel John Boyd captured this strategy in the OODA loop: observe, orient, decide, and act. Buford approached the battlefield through Maryland and ended up on Cemetery Ridge, a prime position on the high ground, giving him an excellent vantage point.

The Civil War placed the enslaved behind enemy lines. Some acted as spies for the Union, aiding troops in any way they could. Slave owners assumed most slaves were ignorant and illiterate, yet slaves helped the Union soldiers trapped behind Confederate lines. They were overlooked in the process yet essential parts of the disruption.

Returning to the battle, according to historian Christopher J. Olsen, "Troops were divided into three branches: infantry, cavalry, and artillery. The infantry was expected to do the bulk of the fighting, supported by the artillery, while the cavalry provided information on the enemy and screened the movement of the infantry in order to confuse the other side." The infantry held off the Confederate troops on horseback. On the ground, the men were stronger and could fight longer. On horses, the cavalry was more visible and they had to tend to wounded animals as well as humans. The cavalry had to provide their own horse, so many of the men hailed from the upper class. This created more divisions, as those on horseback probably had less experience fighting on or off the ground.

Buford's men held the Confederates off until General Reynolds' reinforcements arrived. In terms of the management hierarchy, Col. Vossler said General Reynolds allowed Buford to "lead up." Buford actually led the General with the General's blessing, despite the latter outranking him. Col. Vossler also added that decisiveness is often more important than the content of the decision. Buford and Reynolds didn't have time to deliberate. Reynolds didn't wait for a second, third, or fourth report; he received the relevant information and promptly responded. He trusted Buford. When leaders don't trust others, can you really trust the leader?

Examining the weapons used in the Civil War is also relevant in this discussion regarding perspective. According to Col. Vossler, more Union soldiers bore cavalry sabers and rifles, while more Confederates had muskets. Muskets fired one shell rounds with no spin about 60 yards, while the rifles fired spinning cone-shaped shells accurately about 350 yards. Reloading muskets was a nightmare compared to the fast reloading of the rifles. Technology clearly played a role and the number of deaths was high as a result.

Part of the reason the Union won the Battle of Gettysburg was their ability to innovate. Col. Vossler discussed how Dr. Jonathan Letterman developed a triage system, working on patients based on the severity of the injury. Letterman also created an ambulance system to transport troops, using horse-drawn wagons with springs to cushion the ride. In addition, the U.S. Sanitation Commission built a system to separate human waste from clean drinking water, digging the latrine downstream and not upstream to avoid contaminating their water supply. Diseases were the deadliest enemy during the war, and Dr. Letterman's innovations were literally "life-saving and life-changing."

Most of the Confederate troops did not have experience fighting in a war, while the Union had more immigrants who had fought in previous conflicts. The war was the ultimate act of on the job training. Soldiers paid the price with their lives when leaders were inept. In the twenty-first century, some companies and institutions are being sacrificed for the same reason; rather than losing their lives, they are instead losing their livelihoods.

While the Confederates were sleeping after exhausting battles, the Union worked through the night building barricades. The Union filled in the unmanned and uncontested space. This is what emerging markets allow new entrants to do as Christensen says in *The Innovator's Dilemma*. The inaction of the dominant companies leaves plenty of room for future competitors to prepare for and market to ignored or overlooked consumers.

General Lee ignored the wisdom of General James Longstreet and engaged in a disastrous battle. Longstreet urged Lee to withdraw, but Lee refused. Leaders who won't listen are really managers with titles. Col. Vossler talked about predictable leadership: they do what they know, what they've always done in the past. Lee forced Longstreet to execute a plan when most troops were not in place. General Lee also ignored Longstreet's recommendations when Lee ordered General George E. Pickett to have his troops charge Cemetery Hill, with disastrous results.

In direct contrast, Union General George G. Meade assembled his team, including men of junior rank, and held a war council. He asked them for an assessment of the battlefield, injuries, the health of the men, and other relevant questions. He did not defer to men based on their titles or status; all soldiers in the meeting were allowed to respond. On the UGRR, the playing field of leadership was leveled in a similar fashion. Author Fergus Bordewich states its inherent strength: "Apart from the lives saved, the underground's greatest achievement may have been its creation of interracial activity where blacks not only directed complex logistical and financial operations, but also, in some places, supervised networks that included white men and women who were accorded no special status owing to their skin color." Union officers were more likely to listen to their subordinates than Confederate officers were. General Meade learned of the strengths and weaknesses of his troops, adapting his plans to match the terrain and better circumvent the Confederates.

Meade's open-source style of leadership, not management, may have been the turning point in not just that battle, but in the war. One of the most remarkable facts in my opinion is General John Hooker was relieved of his Union leadership duties by then President Abraham Lincoln three days before the Battle of Gettysburg. Meade was a fresh leader with a unique approach, resulting in the historic outcome. In the digital space, most leaders of new media are young, without years of experience shackling their creativity. Leadership matters, but so does perspective. In Col. Vossler's analysis, General Hooker had his "boys" in positions of power. General Meade relieved incompetent and incapable men of their duties, putting young captains in charge.

Had the Union leadership team disagreed with General Meade, they had the opportunity to express their position. Like Stephen B. Sample advocates in his book, *The Contrarian's Guide to Leadership*, it is critical to allow your team to "think gray." "The key to thinking free is to first allow your mind to contemplate really outrageous ideas, and only subsequently apply the constraints of practicality, practicability, legality, cost, time and ethics." Employees need to be able to brainstorm without being barnstormed. In some organizations, the innovative people and ideas sorely needed are being dismissed, or worse yet, ridiculed. When some agencies and institutions need innovators, idea generators, and change agents, they are hard-pressed to find them. When enslaved Africans tried to work within the system to secure their freedom, they were beaten, maimed, or killed. The disruption took hold outside of the system of slavery.

In his book *Blink*, Malcolm Gladwell shares the experience of the U.S. Joint Forces Command (JFCOM), the group running war games to prepare strategies for battle. They devised the Millennium Challenge, creating a red and a blue team and enlisting the help of real troops from all military branches for participation. The red team was led by Paul Van Riper, a Vietnam veteran and an out-of-the box thinker. He knew that in the midst of a battle it was implausible to weigh all options. This is what is happening in the Internet age: too many are demanding assessment and proof of success in advance. With the changes being so rapid, predictions become less predictable, and chances must be taken. The enslaved and UGRR workers did not know what would succeed; like Van Riper, they just went for it, relying on their wit, wisdom, and wherewithal.

Stephen B. Sample encourages leaders to read the classic texts. Van Riper met Gary Klein, a consultant and author of the book *Sources of Power*. Gladwell shares Van Riper's insight, "...when experts make decisions, they don't logically and systematically compare all available options. That is the way people are taught to make decisions, but in real life it is much too slow."

Klein advocated UGRR conductor Harriet Tubman's practice of following one's experiences and intuition, and that's how the red team operated. Needless to say, the red team soundly trumped the blue team. According to Gladwell, the blue team based their strategy on "databases and matrixes and methodologies for systematically understanding their intentions and capabilities of the enemy." Van Riper said, "Any moderately informed person would know enough not to count on those technologies. That's a Blue Team mind-set."

Gladwell makes it clear that Van Riper's win wasn't a fluke. The ability to make good decisions is based on training, rules, and rehearsals, and Gladwell uses the art of improvisation to highlight his point. In improv, the idea of agreement is "the notion that a very simple way to create a story—or humor—is to have characters accept everything that happens to them." Hit the pause button, this is a TWP (thought worth pondering) moment. Like General Meade, Van Riper empowered his troops to make on-the-spot decisions. In this way, Gladwell says, "allowing people to operate without having to explain themselves constantly turns out to be like the rule of agreement in improv. It enables rapid cognition."

This is how many decisions had to be made on the UGRR. Data wasn't available. The quest for freedom forced the enslaved to examine and change their perspectives. They had to adjust to the thought of being free and leaving what little they had behind them. They left their old thoughts, feelings, and failures behind them in order to move forward. Mindset played a major role in the conflict.

As Daniel Pink asserts in his book *A Whole New Mind,* there needs to be a renewed passion for empathy, story, meaning, play, symphony, and design. The world needs the creativity of the right-brained thinkers since the computer can provide the left-brain information. Enslaved Africans were predominantly right-brained thinkers. They were not indoctrinated in school or by religion. They may have been in chains and their minds were under siege, yet some still exercised freedom of thought. Computers cannot provide context or make connections the way humans can just yet. The right-brained skills are extremely beneficial for indexing and curating data, one of the fastest growing professional areas.

More right-brained thinkers have instantaneous, international access thanks to the Internet. Immigrants often have greater success innovating because they have fewer preconceived notions and are highly motivated. During the Global South Summit in Nashville, Tennessee, author and journalist Thomas Friedman discussed his new book co-authored with Michael Mandelbaum entitled *That Used to Be Us: How America Fell Behind in the World It Invented and How We Can Come Back*. He said young people should think like an artisan, a waitress, a start-up founder, and an immigrant. Regarding thinking like an immigrant, he said they find and figure out opportunities. They are adaptable, paranoid optimists, staying hungry and participating in the interconnected world, operating from a position filled with possibilities. Artisans take pride in their work. They make everything individually, with some even carving their initials in their work. Friedman emphasizes the importance of craftsmanship no matter the project: the ability to multitask while serving people effectively is a desirable skill. Restaurant servers must think like entrepreneurs; they may give a customer an extra piece of fruit and receive a larger tip as a result, for example. A start-up founder realizes their work is never finished, always in a constant process of improvement. More people now have the ability to participate in the free market enterprise. This access cannot be taken for granted. It should not be exploited, underestimated, or compromised. The Internet is a global platform, providing unprecedented access for organization and collaboration.

People who resisted change, refusing to see a different point of view and steadfastly holding onto the past, compromised the country's conscience. In the end, some argue the Civil War was the product of two minority groups: abolitionists and pro-slavery. The majority of citizens didn't voice an opinion, but all became casualties of war. The Underground Railroad was a passionate effort to fight for the soul of the country.

SUMMARY

- Mindset matters.
- The Underground Railroad was a relevant factor leading up to the Civil War, with some arguing it was a catalyst.
- Some Southern states seceded from the Union because of slavery, a concern over states' rights, and a desire for more political power.
- Historically, the political party without the majority in Congress argues for states' rights. They also may ask to limit the power of the federal government.
- The South favored the past. The North focused on the future.
- The Northern and Southern boundaries of free and slave states set the stage for border wars leading up to the Civil War.
- The Emancipation Proclamation did not free all enslaved Africans. It only freed those in Confederate states.
- The 13th Amendment to the Constitution of the United States legally abolished slavery.
- In the Battle at Gettysburg, the perspective of the leaders was the determining factor for success.
- Open source leadership is critical in the twenty-first century.
- Too much can hinder the decision-making process just as much as too little data.

CHAPTER NINE

Pioneering

"Do not fear to pioneer, to venture down new paths of endeavor."

RALPH J. BUNCHE

The Underground Railroad was an elaborate, pioneering network. It was a first on U.S. soil: a leaderless movement, decentralized and always evolving to avoid detection. For this reason, enslaved Africans were often led down different paths to freedom. Like the modern day global positioning system (GPS), guides knew several alternate routes, yet there were many unknown possibilities. This fact made it extremely difficult for slave-catchers to follow, let alone find, missing fugitives. Since an enslaved person was often the first down a path, they were pioneers. Many of the enslaved were the first to leave their plantations and the first to try a new way of escape. This is an essential component in the *Art of War*. In an edited version by Marc A. Moore, he said, "By altering his arrangements and changing his plans, he keeps the enemy without definite knowledge. By shifting his camp and taking circuitous routes, he prevents the enemy from anticipating his purpose." Remember, when people copy HBO, they are not flattered; HBO runs to new territory.

In this vein, the pioneering work of slave-turned-abolitionist John P. Parker should not be forgotten. Parker was born a slave in 1827 in Norfolk,

94

Virginia, and his life was chronicled in *His Promised Land: The Autobiography of John P. Parker, Former Slave and Conductor on the Underground Railroad*, edited by historian Stuart Seely Sprague. As a child, Parker was forced to walk from Virginia to Alabama by a hateful master, and he was eventually sold to a doctor in Mobile, Alabama. Flouting the law, the doctor's sons taught Parker how to read; in return, Parker taught the boys how to fish. He was even sent away to college with the boys until it seemed he would escape; by then, he had already made several attempts. He hated his life in bondage and made up his mind to secure his freedom. He was finally able to purchase his freedom in 1845.

No longer a slave, Parker moved to Ohio, eventually starting a foundry business. He was a pioneer in business, securing patents for several inventions, and was among the few blacks receiving patents before 1900; as noncitizens, enslaved Africans could not legally hold a patent. In addition to being an entrepreneur, Parker was an active participant in the Underground Railroad, helping those seeking freedom cross the Ohio River.

Some innovators are not appreciated, at least not at first; Parker learned this lesson first-hand, sharing this account of working hard and excelling at his craft in his autobiography: "Being of an inventive turn of mind, as you will see later, I soon rigged up my bench so I could do more and better work than any man in the shop. This fact naturally caused some ill feeling among the other workmen towards me." Haters are everywhere. In *Mavericks at Work,* Taylor and LaBarre said, "Sometimes the innovators with the most compelling strategic twists choose to broadcast them with a whisper rather than a shout." A great example is when abolitionist Levi Coffin received a party of more than twenty fugitives. He organized the enslaved Africans into a funeral procession, safely passing them on to the next station. He didn't "shout" his plan; only those who needed to know were informed.

Parker was a family man. In 1848 he married Miranda Boulden, a free Black woman, and the couple had six children, three sons and three daughters. The two oldest sons both went to Oberlin College; Sprague doesn't say where Parker's youngest son attended school, but he eventually became a school principal. All of the Parker girls studied music; the middle daughter, Hortense, was among the first Black graduates at Mount Holyoke in 1883. Parker loved to read, and greatly valued education. Due to his businesses being burned in the middle of the night, he didn't want his children to follow in his footsteps; instead, he made sure they all graduated from college. In his notes for Parker's autobiography, Spague notes that "In just two generations, the Parker family moved from slavery to the college-educated black middle class."

In the book *The Liberty Line*, Larry Gara focuses on the ingenuity and capabilities of the enslaved. Gara was frustrated most historical records discounted or excluded the fugitive and free Blacks' role on the UGRR as well as in emancipating slaves in general. He also did not like the way the UGRR was romanticized, making it difficult to discern fact from fiction. This is the reason why so many examples are cited to support claims in this research. Like James W. Loewen in *Lies My Teacher Told Me*, Gara attempts to balance and correct inaccuracies and oversights in numerous UGRR accounts.

Gara confirms, "It was the gifted and highly intelligent slave who enjoyed semi-freedom as a hired laborer and having greater sophistication and more freedom of movement, was better qualified than most bondsman to conceive and put into action a plan of escape." Enslaved Africans were not lazy. Some used their free time to work to earn extra money to attempt to purchase their freedom. According to the late historian John Hope Franklin, "Lunsford Lane of Raleigh, for example, spent his spare time making pipes, raising chickens, and engaging in other tasks in order to realize his ambition of becoming free." Lane's friend did the same and still was forced to runaway when his owner reneged on his promise to free him. Many had their funds stolen by unscrupulous slave owners, catchers, and or traders.

According to Christopher J. Olsen in *The American Civil War*, "The vast majority of fugitives were young, single men; most came from border-states or upper South; and most hid in Northern cities among the free population of color." The enslaved attempting escape primarily traveled during the night to see the North Star, during the winter, on weekends, and on holidays, sleeping during the day. By definition, innovators are pioneers, willing to be called crazy, different, and downright wrong, and the enslaved endured the most vile language and circumstances to try different approaches to secure their freedom.

Henry "Box" Brown was yet another enslaved African turned pioneer. He had a friend, Samuel A. Smith, place him in a box and ship him from Richmond, Virginia, to Philadelphia, Pennsylvania. Brown was so determined to be free, he allowed himself to be placed in a box. That's definitely a thought worth pondering (TWP) moment. In his book recalling experiences on the UGRR, William Still noted that it was "Two feet eight inches deep, two feet wide, and three feet long were the exact dimensions of the box, lined with baize (a cheap cloth)... (with) One bladder of water and a few small biscuits." There was one sizeable hole placed in the encasement for air. Brown's ordeal took twenty-six hours. Because of this success, Samuel S. Smith attempted to send two more fugitives in separate boxes, but they were captured and Smith was arrested.

The UGRR didn't exist as an official network, but the Internet does. The Internet is the first network to provide the infrastructure for innovation on an unprecedented scale. The barrier of entry has been dramatically lowered, giving people greater access to create and to innovate. It has allowed people to create alternatives to existing business structures, such as when Shawn Fanning, John Fanning, and Sean Parker created Napster, a peer-to-peer network (p2p) that severely disrupted the music industry by allowing consumers to download and share music for free. The recording industry sued the company and won, shutting it down. Harvard Professor Yochai Benkler, author of *The Wealth of Networks: How Social Production Transforms Markets and Freedom,* describes p2p: "Technically, p2p networks are algorithms that run on top of the Internet and allow users to connect directly from one end user's machine to another. In theory, that is how the whole Internet works—or at least how it worked when there were a small number of computers attached to it." Legal action isn't a viable long-term strategy when new companies emerge every day. Napster, KaZaa, and Grokster disrupted the music industry, while overseas operations like the Pirate Bay have done the same for the film industry. As Matt Mason asserts in *The Pirate's Dilemma,* innovating may be the most viable option for any industry dealing with piracy. Their economic health depends on it.

The economic system of the twenty-first century is a networked economy. It is based on connection, collaboration, and community. Professor

Benkler says that "decentralized individual action" is a characteristic of the networked information economy. He goes on to say within the network those actions are cooperative and coordinated without a need for management and control. People are self-sufficient. They can create relationships, products, or anything else without asking permission or needing extensive oversight to do so. I wrote "UGRR" in the margins after reading this assessment. These are the very same characteristics evident on the pioneering network.

In a networked economy, free flowing information appears to lead to a more profitable outcome long term. Creative Commons provides six different ways to license your work online. It is an experimental alternative to copyright in the U.S. For example, you can allow others to use your work as long as they give you credit for it. Or you may not allow others to make money from your work. Again, connecting the past to the present, the enslaved and their supporters created a system to secure their freedom. They did not limit who could use their innovative ideas to escape. One fugitive could use part of another person's escape route. It was innovative, pioneering, and unimaginable at the time.

In his book *Drive*, Daniel Pink stresses the importance of autonomy, another word for freedom. He discusses the results-only work environment (ROWE) created by Cali Ressler and Jody Thompson, former human resources leaders at Best Buy. In the ROWE system, people don't have schedules; instead, they have assignments to complete, without being micromanaged. They are empowered and trusted to complete the task in a set period of time, allowing employees to maximize their time. The ROWE concept led me straight to the UGRR. The enslaved traveled when it was best for them and/or for their agents and conductors. The Internet makes the ROWE type of autonomy possible since the network can be accessed remotely. This freedom creates greater loyalty among some employees. They are less likely to leave the employer even when offered more money to join a competitor. Their freedom is priceless. This is exactly how fugitives left the plantation and how conductors helped transport slaves on the UGRR. Guides did not act ruthlessly and impose time or location constraints like overseers. Modern day managers would be wise to act as facilitators and not overseers, promoting decentralized individual action and leveraging the strengths of the individual. Research confirms productivity increases under ROWE situations. Yup, it's a TWP moment.

In *The Pirate's Dilemma*, Matt Mason says, "A pirate is essentially anyone who broadcasts or copies someone else's creative property without paying for it or obtaining permission." Let that sink in for a minute, then reread that a few times, thinking about all those who have had their work stolen from them. Corporations cry foul when their profits are affected, but when the shoe is on the other foot, they just keep on walking. A prime example is the music industry.

In the early 1990s, Prince was often seen in public with the word "slave" on his face. While at the time many thought he was crazy, ungrateful, or just being Prince, he was protesting for his artistic freedom and asserting his rights. He was spending his entire life working, but not making his fair share of the money he was making for other people. Now, Prince owns his name, his brand, his music, and his destiny, keeping the lion's share of the profits he generates and calling his own shots. He is one of a few artists whose work is not being pirated on a large scale online; a possible reason for this is that he gives it away. In the summer of 2007, he really made some in the recording industry unhappy when he gave away millions of copies of his *Planet Earth* CD. It was a genius strategy, using *The Long Tail* author Chris Anderson's free business model, giving away the CDs and simultaneously selling out all of his European concerts.

On the Underground Railroad, there wasn't a way to analyze, assess, or measure the success of the network at that time. By its very nature, the network had to be free from regulation in order to help change regulations. The Internet must remain free until it matures, otherwise its growth may be permanently stunted. Again, this is the point James A. Dewar made to RAND. Likewise, many industries need to figure out how to provide their consumers with greater opportunities for participation as well as customization. The UGRR was able to spread because it was difficult to prove that it even existed. Person-to-person contacts were an essential part of that effort.

To revisit the digital vernacular, guides were like GPS systems. They had to navigate and make decisions quickly based on their experiences and instincts, and they couldn't leave a trace. Online, small files called cookies are left behind for certain websites to track your behavior; for example, Amazon tracks your browsing history in order to recommend merchandise for purchases. If the enslaved left any symbols and signals, they were covert. Again, online, sins may be forgiven but they will never be forgotten.

A "free" market should be free of manipulation and domination. The Internet is an open, collaborative space where risks can be taken and new initiatives should be pioneered. In some ways, the current system of ownership is antiquated and ineffective. Copyright laws have not benefited the overall economic system in a significant way. This is a big TWP moment. Professor Yochai Benkler says, "...there is remarkably little support in economics for regulating information, knowledge, and cultural production through the tools of intellectual property law." He argues innovation that comes from non-market sources and producers who operate outside of the "regulatory framework of intellectual property," meaning those who are free of certain constraints due to operating outside of a gated structure, faring better in a networked economy. There isn't a significant reward for creating scarcity through the system of copyright. Some are making more money now because information is more easily accessed, purchased, and shared. The financial incentive to work within the system is diminishing in some industries. Innovation is placed squarely on the shoulders of risk-takers, fringe players, and pioneers operating outside of existing systems.

Benkler notes that Hollywood, the recording industry, and pharmaceutical companies clearly have a vested interest in the system of control through intellectual property. But Benkler argues that a walled, closed, or exclusive networked economy defeats the purpose in the digital age. It is the age of sharing, customization, and personalization. Making consumers play by outdated rules is forcing many companies out of business. More and more businesses and people are not relying on controlled systems, instead collaborating in a networked, open-source economy, one that allows people to share and build on each other's ideas.

Author Matt Mason notes this innovative openness has worked well in the fashion world. "Freedom to copy other people's designs is taken for granted in the world of fashion, which makes it unusual, but it's also the reason it's so successful." And like Benkler, Mason believes an open system must be embraced to capitalize on collaboration and to neutralize the pirates. "When regulations and patents are stifling our economies, our environment, and even human life itself, individuals and entire nations have responded with the pirate mentality, raising the stakes with world-changing consequences." Laws legally enslaved people nearly four hundred years ago. The UGRR appeared to combat that injustice.

In America, it isn't a secret many ideas have been taken without permission. In *The Pirate's Dilemma*, Matt Mason provides many substantive examples of this reality. Steve Jobs once said, "Picasso had a saying—'good artists copy, great artists steal'—and we have always been shameless about stealing great ideas." The difference here is that when the enslaved left the plantation, they weren't "stealing" their freedom for financial gain.

The innovations on the UGRR were truly pioneering. In *Let My People Go*, Henrietta Buckmaster describes several creative projects: "False closets through trap doors in kitchens or parlors, false cupboards over brick ovens, sliding panels by fireplaces where wood was stowed, secret rooms without windows—these became 'stations' on the underground route." Of course, all escapes weren't successful or simple; in 1834, despite several safe houses scattered throughout various communities, a runaway slave from Tennessee, Jarm Logue, couldn't find one when he escaped with a fellow slave. Author Larry Gara tells Logue's story: "Actually, they got very little aid and were cheated badly when they sold their horse to a Quaker. For the rest of the trip they thought it prudent not to make inquiries; so they trusted the North Star and eventually reached their goal." Once free, Logue learned to read, became a minister, and changed his name to Jermain Wesley Loguen. He ran a successful station on the Underground Railroad in Syracuse, New York. Because of its proximity to Canada, Syracuse was not only a pivotal point on the Underground Railroad, but a hotbed of anti-slavery activity.

Loguen, along with many others, participated in the Jerry Rescue, a public effort to help fugitive slave William Henry (nicknamed "Jerry"). According to Bordewich, Jerry had escaped from slavery in Missouri and settled in Syracuse, and was at work making barrels when he was arrested under the Fugitive Slave Act of 1850. The Liberty Party, staunch abolitionists, were holding their state convention in Syracuse, and word of Jerry's arrest soon spread like wildfire. A crowd soon formed and rushed the police station, rescuing Jerry by force; he was then able to escape to Canada via the Underground Railroad. Twenty-six people were indicted as a result of the rescue, but there was only a single conviction. Several people fled to Canada to avoid being convicted, including Loguen.

When the enslaved were running for freedom, they didn't have a choice. They had to take a chance, to be pioneers. They took many different routes to freedom; if overseers found out about one route, they adjusted and went another. The free Blacks and abolitionists who aided them had to do the same. When people are backed up against the wall and told what they can and cannot do, which way they can and cannot go, what service they will and must use, the price they are to pay, then the stage is set for a revolt, online and off. Passions run deep when freedom and innovation are involved.

SUMMARY

- The Underground Railroad was a pioneering network, a first of its kind.

- Slave-turned-abolitionist John Parker helped fugitives cross the Ohio River near Ripley, Ohio. Parker was a business owner and one of the first Blacks in America to secure a patent.

- The enslaved Africans most likely to attempt escape were intelligent, skilled, and tended to have greater freedoms through additional employment away from their plantations.

- Henry "Box" Brown was shipped in a box from Virginia to Pennsylvania to secure his freedom.

- Like the pirates disrupting the music industry, the enslaved disrupted the slave enterprise. Pirates respond to injustices in existing systems.

- A networked economy allows for the free flow of ideas and information.

- Research proves the effectiveness of the results-only work environment.

- The UGRR had to remain free from existing systems to realize its potential. Some argue the Internet needs the same autonomy to fully develop.

- Some of the enslaved Africans preferred death than life as a slave.

Passion

"Passion is the genesis of genius."

TONY ROBBINS

Passion drives innovation. How did Underground Railroad conductor Harriet Tubman and others persuade some slaves to buy into the idea of escaping for freedom? Why did some enslaved Africans choose to escape while others did not? The decisions to leave the plantation through the Underground Railroad was, to a large extent, an internal one; external motivators like fear of abuse or of a family being separated were certainly factors, but the true motivation to participate in the UGRR, whether enslaved or free, came from within. Those who supported escaped slaves shared a passion for freedom. The Cincinnati, Ohio region was a pivotal place for the UGRR. It was there that a small, yet determined, group united and helped change the course of history. Whether on the tracks, in the churches, or in educational institutions, passionate people came together for the cause of freedom.

Lane Theological Seminary, founded in Cincinnati in 1829, was the location for an epic, eighteen-night debate on slavery, ranging from topics such as immediatism (releasing slaves immediately) and the merits of the

American Colonization Society (who proposed sending freed slaves to the new African colony of Liberia). In *Beyond the River,* Ann Hagedorn shares this account from a student who lived in the South and had witnessed slavery's brutality first-hand, relating the story at the debates: "At our house it is common to hear their screams from a neighboring plantation, that we think nothing of it. The overseer of this plantation told me one day that he laid a woman over a log and beat her so severely that she soon after delivered a dead baby." Disturbing accounts like these swayed the hearts of many in the audience, leading several students to organize an abolitionist group. Fearing Southern rage, the Seminary trustees panicked and banned the anti-slavery society on campus. Some took this as an affront to their right to free speech, and at least thirty students left, eventually enrolling at Oberlin College. Youth movements can be very disruptive.

Matt Mason says, "Youth cultures often embody some previously invisible, unacknowledged feeling in society and give it an identity." According to Erik Qualman's Social Media Revolution video on YouTube, more than fifty percent of the world's population is under the age of thirty. Many who participated in the Arab Spring uprisings are from this generation. Youth movements are often ignored initially. Mason uses the rise of hip-hop to illustrate this point: "Increasingly, when new forms of youth culture survive, it's because they are things the media wouldn't touch with a ten-foot pole—this was very much the case with hip-hop at its inception, for example. With everything from urban legends to conversations with our neighbors about detergents becoming a carefully placed marketing message, it's only at the outer limits of acceptability in society that grassroots movements can find meaning." Some forms of hip-hop may offend, but the core of the movement gives back to the community. "Anyone can be a part of hip-hop, anyone can borrow it, but nobody can own it. It is defined by participation and collaboration." No rules, no boundaries. This sounds a lot like the UGRR.

Enslaved Africans were forced to use their intuition and experiential knowledge. Apple pioneer Steve Jobs chose to use his experience and inner voice no matter what. According to Walter Isaacson, Jobs' biographer, Jobs embraced this maxim from scientist Alan Kay: "The best way to predict the future is to invent it." Jobs made people believe they could accomplish the impossible. Agents and conductors on the UGRR had to instill this same belief in timid fugitives. The most passionate conductors were arguably more successful. When Jobs hired people, passion wasn't optional.

Jobs believed in many maxims, including "don't compromise" and "it's not done until it ships." These tenets were readily apparent on the UGRR. Marketer and author Seth Godin talks at length about the idea of shipping in his book about linchpins. "The only purpose of starting is to finish, and while the projects we do are never really finished, they must ship." (Thus, with much fear and trembling, this book has been published) Godin goes on to say, "Shipping something out the door, doing it regularly, without hassle, emergency, or fear—this is a rare skill, something that makes you indispensable." Some of the enslaved were passionate, indispensable linchpins. "The linchpin is able to invent a future, fall in love with it, live in it—and then abandon it on a moment's notice." That's simply what pioneering innovators do.

To some, fear may be death by a dozen doubts, and some innovators face virtual death each day they go to work. Steve Jobs refused to allow doubt to impede progress: "What drove me? I think most creative people want to express appreciation for being able to take advantage of the work that's been done by others before us. We try to use the talents we have to express our deep feelings, to show our appreciation of all the contributions that came before us, and to add something to that flow. That's what has driven me." Now that's passion, but in the twenty-first century, fear and passion are often at odds. Godin put it this way: "Now, though, the economy is forcing us to confront this fear. The economy is ruthlessly punishing the fearful, and increasing the benefits to the few who are brave enough to create art and generous enough to give it away." This is what many abolitionists on the UGRR accomplished. They leveraged their passion to face their fears and help thousands of strangers along the way.

Laura Haviland was one of those brave people, and the subject of Mildred Danforth's book *A Quaker Pioneer: Laura Haviland, Superintendent of the Underground*. Though born a Quaker, she and her husband eventually joined the Methodist Church over differing positions on slavery; while some Quakers had freed their slaves, they did not wish to fight for their gradual or immediate emancipation, while Haviland was more active than many preferred. She and her husband Charles settled in Raisin, Michigan. Laura Haviland was passionate about education and about helping the enslaved. She worked with her brother, Harvey, a student at Oberlin College, to start the Raisin Institute, despite verbal assaults her and being ostracized her for her efforts. She was even known to travel with escaping slaves, escorting them to freedom, and often aided other abolitionists in the fight for freedom. This is where her path is connected to another well-known abolitionist: Calvin Fairbank.

Fairbank, a White Methodist preacher and former Oberlin College student, was known to help fugitive slaves. When he learned that a slave named Gilson Berry wanted to rescue his wife, Fairbank volunteered to do the job. Fairbank had to go to Lexington, Kentucky and enlisted the help of a friend, Delia Webster of Vermont, to complete the mission. Though unsuccessful because the slave's wife did not meet them, Fairbank and Webster did rescue three other slaves: Lewis Hayden, his wife, and his son in 1844.

When Fairbank and Webster returned to Kentucky, they were arrested for their participation in the Haydens' escape. Fairbank was sentenced to fifteen years in prison (five years for each slave), while Webster served two months of a two-year sentence. While in prison, Fairbank reached out to Laura Haviland, who visited him and brought him various supplies. She had discouraged him from attempting to rescue the enslaved. Haviland, like Coffin, didn't believe in going to plantations enticing the enslaved to freedom. Fairbank was released after four years (after Hayden had paid the debt owed to his former master, thereby earning Fairbank's freedom as well), but two years later, Fairbank was imprisoned once again for aiding an escaping slave. His treatment while in jail was brutal, but was eventually pardoned by the Acting Governor of Kentucky during the Civil War.

Another passionate abolitionist was Jonathan Walker, a shipwright and tradesman living in Pensacola, Florida. Growing up poor, he empathized with the enslaved; when he was asked to escort several escapees to the Bahamas, he gladly obliged. At the time, the Bahamas were a British colony, and the British had abolished slavery in 1833, making the country an ideal destination for those too far south to safely make the trip to Canada. Unfortunately, Walker fell ill shortly after embarking on the trip, and the fleeing slaves had no nautical experience; they were found by another ship and taken back to Florida, where Walker was promptly arrested. As part of his punishment, his right hand was branded "SS" for "slave stealer." Walker was lauded as a hero in the abolitionist community, and as word of his ordeal spread, it served to only strengthen the abolitionist movement.

Movements begin with passion. Someone sees a problem and makes a commitment to solve it. There is a connection between passion and movements leading to action, innovation. Recall Everett Roger's definition of innovation: an idea, practice, or object that is perceived as new by an individual or other unit of adoption. The key was the ability of enslaved Africans to seek freedom and to use the Underground Railroad as a viable option to aid escape. Running for freedom crossed the minds of many of the enslaved, and there were many bodies buried to prove it. However, the innovation was the coordinated passion of the conductors and stationmasters who played a critical role. Collective action isn't always easy to coordinate, and without modern technology or government support, those involved in the UGRR facilitated an effective "collective action" to wage an informal battle against slavery.

Moore's edited version of Sun Tzu's *The Art of War* has several lines that are relevant to a discussion of the battle waged by UGRR participants. "All warfare is deception. Hence, when able to attack, we must seem unable." Some of the enslaved pretended to be ignorant; when they knew how to read, they never let their overseers know it. "When using our forces, we must seem inactive." An enslaved African may have appeared to be asleep, but was actually reviewing their escape plan. "When we are near, we must make the enemy believe we are far away." Fugitives often hid close by because their owners couldn't imagine a slave being so bold; after all, if they were escaping, why wouldn't they try to get as far away as possible?

Passion forces innovation and inspires creativity. Like the Underground Railroad, the Internet provides a means for production and distribution. And because of the scale of the digital system, something small can make a huge impact. In *The Long Tail,* author Chris Anderson describes how small things, when added together, can become big. It's not about the best-selling book or the number one song, it's about the demand for the supply at the other end of the pipeline. Anderson says, "popularity no longer has a monopoly on profitability."

In the digital world, shelf space is infinite. In the print edition of newspapers or on television, space and time are limited. Being able to store as many digital files as needed changes the game. A physical location is no longer necessary either; packages can be shipped directly to the customer. You can connect customers with things they typically cannot find, and you can partner with other stores and companies to do it. This is another game-changer. The UGRR seemed bigger than it was because it used extra capacity and capitalized on outsourcing. In *The World is Flat,* journalist Thomas Friedman shows how companies like Papa John's Pizza are doing the same by partnering with other businesses like UPS for delivery services.

Not all who are passionate about their work are formally trained for their tasks; amateurs often put in more hours than professionals. According to Malcolm Gladwell in his book *Outliers*, psychologists have found the "magic number" of hours spent building your expertise to be ten thousand; it takes approximately ten years of progressive skill building to accumulate that much time. The Beatles were together for seven years before the "British Invasion." They built their stamina and improved their skills playing non-stop for hours at clubs in Hamburg, Germany. Their passion for music changed them from amateurs to professionals, and audiences let them know when they had arrived. Quality is in the eye (or ear) of the consumer.

In *The Long Tail*, Chris Anderson shows how some amateurs are more passionate than professionals. Most amateurs are motivated internally, while most professionals are motivated externally. However, amateurs are more likely to have fun and a vested interest in a common goal, whether there is financial gain involved or not. It's this passion that powers innovation.

Amateurs and professionals worked together on the UGRR. In regards to the Internet, Clay Shirky broke it down this way in his book, *Here Comes Everybody:* "With the arrival of globally accessible publishing, freedom of speech is now freedom of press, and freedom of the press is freedom of assembly." With the growth of the Internet, virtually anything is possible; marrying innovative ideas with passion leads to amazing results.

In *The Wisdom of the Crowds*, James Surowiecki stresses the importance of diversity, independence, and decentralization. With relation to innovation, he says, "You want diversity among the entrepreneurs who are coming up with the ideas, so you end up with meaningful differences among those ideas rather than minor variations on the same concept." He goes on to say that if all people with power are alike, decision-making is negatively affected. Democracy is strengthened by diversity.

When assessing the abilities of enslaved Africans, the slave owners were blinded by ignorance. In the book *Blink*, Malcolm Gladwell remarked, "They stopped relying on the actual evidence of their senses and fell back on a rigid and unyielding system, a stereotype." In order to change their perspectives, they would have to change their surroundings. Gladwell argues getting to know people of other ethnicities, religions, or creeds "requires that you change your life so that you are exposed to minorities (or whoever the unknown group may be) on a regular basis and become comfortable with them and familiar with the best of their culture, so that when you want to meet, hire, date, or talk with a member of a minority, you aren't betrayed by your hesitation or discomfort." In a world that is flat, this is not an optional skill. Friedman says, "The more you have a culture that naturally glocalizes—that is, the more your culture easily absorbs foreign ideas and best practices and melds those with its own traditions—the greater advantage you will have in a flat world."

The UGRR was a decentralized, diverse, and independent network, dependent on the "wisdom of the crowd." The enslaved worked with free Blacks as well as White abolitionists, coordinating with each other and finding out who knew what, who could be trusted, and who had the latest escape route. It didn't matter who provided the information, just that it was accurate.

The conductors, agents, and routes of the Underground Railroad were interchangeable. It was an amazing dynamic, especially without a central leader. Their passion for freedom drove their efforts, which in turn encouraged flexibility; it was easier to adjust because there wasn't a standard way of doing things on the UGRR. In *Disrupting Class*, Clayton Christenten and his fellow authors discuss the flexibility of modular systems. Modularity allows different parts to come together in an open, collaborative way. This is how the UGRR operated. Today, connections are being made across counties, communities, and countries.

As the world is being "commodified" for the commercialization of entertainment, Economist Jeremy Rifkin predicts in a century, English will be "all pervasive." In *Dan Poynter's Self-Publishing Manual*, Poynter observes that people only use "800 to 1000 of the approximately 26,000 English words available to them." This is eerily similar to George Orwell's book *1984*, where "newspeak" was a reduced vocabulary of only about 200 words, allowing the government total control over its people. Language isn't the only thing being standardized. On one of Steve Jobs' vacations, he visited Turkey and he made this relevant observation about the younger generation: "It hit me that, for young people, this whole world is the same now. When we're making products, there is no such thing as a Turkish phone, or a music player that young people in Turkey would want that's different from one young people elsewhere would want. We're just one world now." Yes, it's another TWP moment. This may seem off-track as it relates to the UGRR. It is not. My mind sees the potential threat universal uniformity will have on freedom and another UGRR may emerge as a result.

"Losing access to the rich cultural diversity of thousands of years of lived experience would be as devastating to our future ability to survive and flourish as losing our remaining biological diversity," writes Jeremy Rifkin in *The Age of Access*. Freedom and diversity are worth a passionate fight. On the Underground Railroad, passion provided an energy through which the system could thrive. Innovation and passion are intrinsically tied; it is difficult to have one without the other. On the UGRR, those who participated could not ignore the internal drive to do so; individuals like Laura Haviland, Harriet Tubman, Levi Coffin said it was a divine calling. Whatever it was, it wouldn't let them hold their peace until freedom was won for all people. It was very serious business.

SUMMARY

- Passion cannot be contained.
- Youth movements play a critical role in the fight for freedom.
- The ability to answer one's inner voice marks an exceptional innovator.
- Some White abolitionists sacrificed life and limb to secure justice for all.
- Unpaid amateurs often work harder than paid professionals.
- Diversity strengthens democracy.
- Never underestimating one's opponent is a sign of maturity in leadership.
- Passion is the force helping many to face their fears.

CHAPTER ELEVEN

Play

"Play the game for more than you can afford to lose...

only then will you learn the game."

WINSTON CHURCHILL

Clearly, the UGRR was not a game, but a strategic effort using game dynamics. Some innovations will involve elements of play, occurring or implemented with a carefree spirit. The stress of creating something for a specific outcome is removed, replaced instead with the natural order of experimentation for fun. In his book *A Whole New Mind*, Daniel Pink argues the need for more creative, right brain thinking. Like Chris Anderson in *The Long Tail*, Pink also notes the shift from scarcity to abundance. This abundance has not added to a collective "happiness." Pink contends that in addition to the lack of happiness, abundance (more access to more resources), Asia (more workers, better prepared, pay less), and automation (shift from manpower to computer power) forces individuals and companies to search for meaning. Recall his six aptitudes for future success: design, story, meaning, empathy, symphony, and play.

Some people really enjoy laughing. It's that plain and simple. It's a contagious form of play yielding amazing results. People who laugh a lot live longer, happier lives. Being free to laugh and to play are critical to innovation; creativity can be stifled by being under pressure to produce. Having a ticking clock for motivation is fine, yet having an overseer (oops, I mean a manager) pushing for completion may not be productive. In *The Age of Access*, Jeremy Rifkin says, "Play is what people do when they create culture. It is the letting free of the human imagination to create shared meanings. Play is a fundamental category of human behavior without which civilization could not exist." It is a critical element of some innovation as well, and according to Pink, play isn't an optional skill; he quotes Pat Kane from *The Play Ethic*: "Play will be to the 21st century what work was to the last 300 years of industrial society—our dominant way of knowing, doing and creating value." Pink also uses games as an example of necessary play.

Gaming is a serious business built on the desire to play. Digital gaming will gross more than $70 billion in 2013. Understanding the role of play to create something new or perceived to be new is not an option. In *Reality is Broken*, Jane McGonigal identifies four defining traits of a game: a goal, rules, a feedback system, and voluntary participation. When Henry Brown was shipped in a box from Virginia to Pennsylvania, the plan involved risk, time, a specified goal, and other elements of gaming. On the UGRR, the goal was clear: freedom for enslaved Africans and for all citizens to have a democratic impact on the political process.

In gaming, there is a common goal, understood and agreed upon by the players. As a part of innovation, the element of play affords a childlike freedom and innocence to use instinct and common sense to create. On the UGRR, there weren't any official rules, and the feedback loop was continuous. Conductors, enslaved Africans, strangers, free Blacks, abolitionists, and even slave catchers and owners (in their own, unintentional way) provided valuable information for an escapee. For the most part, the fugitives leaving plantations faced obstacles and often raced against the clock in the form of weather as well as night turning to day. Their ultimate reward was making it to safety.

Futurist Jane McGonigal argues that games make us happy because they are engaging and lead to more positive thinking and experiences. Most people don't want to work. When given a choice, they will choose play, working only because they have to. Some young people do not want to work; they want to live. The Millennial Generation watched their parents divorce and their grandparents lose their jobs; they don't want to sign up for misery, they want to live in an apartment with their friends, work different jobs, and travel. Some cannot purchase a home because their student loan debt is too high. They want to make a difference in the world, helping people and having fun, not to make money just to give it to bill collectors.

Leveraging workers to make someone else wealthy was the premise of the slave system. In *The American Civil War*, Christopher J. Olsen says, "In all social systems there must be a class to do the menial duties, to perform the drudgery of life." Without it, he argues, "you would not have that other class which leads progress, civilization, and refinement." So do you really wonder why young people would rather play? Adults are playing, too. Rifkin describes the notion of "mature play." "Mature play brings people together into shared community. It is both the most intimate and the most sophisticated form of human communication that exists. Mature play is also the antidote to the unbridled exercise of institutional power, be it political or commercial in nature." This concept was embodied in the spirit of the UGRR, a strategic network to thwart the unjust system.

McGonigal inspired some of Seth Priebatsch's work. In his TED Talk, he discussed seven game theory dynamics, going into detail about for specific dynamics: the appointment dynamic, status and influence, progression, and communal discovery. All were evident on the UGRR.

When people have a certain time to be at a certain place for an incentive and/or reward, this is an appointment dynamic. When families would sit at the dinner table and watch the evening news, it was a set appointment. Some fugitives on the UGRR had to meet agents at certain times; this was especially true when they had to cross a bodies of water like the Ohio River. They could not make every appointment due to circumstances beyond their control, but they made every effort to make it to the train depot on time.

Status and influence play on the human desire for recognition. Conductors on the UGRR took pride in making sure their schedules ran on time and their passengers arrived safely. There was a respect for and among dependable participants. Similarly, some programmers and coders relish the praise they receive for solving difficult problems. They may donate their time because they are committed to the cause. It's part of what Chris Anderson and others call the "gift" or "reputation" economy. The gift economy provides intangible rewards in the form of job offers and peer respect.

From a psychological perspective, these rewards are greater than money to some people. They are more pleased with the feeling of accomplishing a goal for its own sake, and some relish victories won through a team effort. In a truly open system, no one takes the credit for collaborative initiatives. This is yet another way the UGRR and the Internet are similar. For the most part, no one was compensated for serving on the UGRR, and many, if not most, will never receive the recognition they deserve. However, the lasting legacies of Harriet Tubman, Levi Coffin, John Rankin, John Parker, William Still, David Ruggles, Frederick Douglass, Laura Haviland, and so many others is a testament to their collective contributions.

Part of the satisfaction on the UGRR was the participants' abilities to contribute more and more to the network. Some ministers would share the cause with church members, join or host meetings for the anti-slavery society, take fugitives to the next safe house, or allow them to stay in their homes. In gaming, the concept of "leveling up" refers to earning more points to achieve a higher level; this is progression. Gamers accomplish a number of tasks and are promoted for their efforts. Priebatsch uses the professional networking site LinkedIn as an example of the desire for progression. If your status isn't one hundred percent, your goal is to reach one hundred percent.

Seth Priebatsch defines communal discovery as "a dynamic wherein an entire community is rallied to work together to solve a challenge." He goes on to say that it leverages the network that is society. The Underground Railroad is a prime example for this. Collaboration is an integral part of communal discovery, one that requires cooperating, coordinating, and co-creating. In gaming, collaboration is absolutely essential for an epic win, which Jane McGonigal defines as "a come-from-behind victory, an unorthodox strategy that works out spectacularly well, a team effort that goes much better than planned, a heroic effort from the most unlikely player." This describes the success, impact, and effectiveness of the Underground Railroad. It assembled an unlikely group of players to face a seemingly insurmountable task.

Psychologist Abraham Maslow created the hierarchy of needs: physiological, the need for food, water, and sleep; safety, the need for employment, health, and resources; love and belonging, the need for friends, family, and intimacy; esteem, the need for accomplishment, confidence, and respect; and finally, self-actualization, the need for creativity, problem solving, and being free from prejudice. In my mind, the most critical need is for a sense of belonging. If this one need is not properly met, people will sacrifice their health by not eating, their self-esteem can be negatively affected, and they cannot become who they were created to be. Author and blogger Jeff Jarvis says something similar in What Would Google Do: what people want most is to be missed. In the gaming community, players are missed especially when their duty is not performed and the team has to pick up the slack. The internet facilitates greater communication and collaboration, and the feeling of belonging can be addressed by personal connections over networks like Vine, Instagram, Pheed, Facebook, Twitter, or the next "big" social media tool. Gaming can help people coordinate and accomplish much good and provide them a necessary escape from reality.

On the UGRR, enslaved Africans had to escape their realities but didn't have technology to assist their efforts. In the digital age, augmented reality provides additional information in the form of graphics, text, audio, and video on top of the real world. For example, if you download the mobile application Layar and search for Black history, in certain cities such as Philadelphia or Boston, you will see information about what historical events happened there on top of your camera's view of what is in front of you. The data comes from the Mobile Black History Project, led by Retha Hill, the Executive Director of the New Media Innovation Lab at Arizona State University. Just imagine if the enslaved had this type of technology at their disposal.

Some confuse augmented reality with virtual reality. In virtual reality, players are immersed in the game via avatars or other interactive means. Real-life doesn't exist in this universe. Alternate reality, on the other hand, involves real people being influenced by other real people and situations. This one is the most difficult to define. It is social and involves people interacting with the real and virtual worlds.

As McGonigal builds her case for using games as an international platform to solve real world problems, she defines alternate reality games as "games played in real life in order to enjoy it [life] more." These games are not designed to help players escape reality, but are engineered to help participants positively engage in a real experience; for example, a game to encourage family members to do their chores. Gaming is an open network. It is taking root outside of most professional systems. Some industries are incorporating games and or game dynamics, but with the growth being so rapid, and in some cases still under the radar, many companies may miss this virtual opportunity.

Although neither Priebatsch nor McGonigal discuss strategy in-depth, it is an extremely relevant game dynamic. Strategy and deception was key on the UGRR. Using deception to attain freedom wasn't ideal, but it was certainly necessary. In Moore's adaptation of *The Art of War*, he says, "Knowing the place and the time of the coming battle, we may concentrate from the greatest distances in order to fight." This distance afforded some of the enslaved the chance to strategize, catching some slave owners and catchers off guard. Most did not know when an enslaved African would escape. Slave catchers monitored borderlands, areas where free and slave states met, they did not know who or where the enemy was. Therefore, it made it extremely difficult for them to identify UGRR participants.

Underestimating one's opponent can lead to devastating results, whether in play, war, or in life. The book *Incidents in the Life of a Slave Girl* describes the first-hand experiences of a slave named Harriet Jacobs. Jacobs was on the run to escape a prominent physician who sexually assaulted her; his daughter was Harriet's legal owner. Jacobs decided to run to avoid being raped the rest of her life. During her seven years as a fugitive, she lived in her grandmother's attic with the aid of her family. Harriet Jacobs said:

> "A small shed had been added to my grandmother's house years ago. Some boards were laid across the joists at the top, and between these boards and the roof was a very small garret, never occupied by any thing but rats and mice. It was a pent roof, covered with nothing but shingles, according to the southern custom for such buildings. The garret was only nine feet long and seven wide. The highest part was three feet high, and sloped down abruptly to the loose board floor. There was no admission for either light or air."

The shed was an innovative creation built by her uncle and her brother. For years, the doctor attempted to find her. In the end, she barely escaped to the North by boat.

In *Beyond the River,* Ann Hagedorn mentions the experience of John Hudson, a free slave in the Gist community in Ohio. Hudson worked with Dr. Isaac Beck and John Mahan to offer assistance to runaways. Mahan connected John Rankin and Levi Coffin on the UGRR. Dr. Beck and Mahan actually raised money to pay John Hudson for his heroic efforts. "Hudson was the man who Mahan, Beck, and Rankin knew could always be depended upon to help run off slave hunters, and who often hid runaway slaves at the Gist camps—an increasingly dangerous scheme, because slave hunters were drawn to free black communities like hounds to the scent." While freeing one fugitive, Hudson followed behind tooting a conch shell to warn the slave his captors were near. "When asked if he was not afraid to arouse the hunter's wrath, he said, No. The knots on the shell would hurt a fellow's head very bad." Humor is a form of play.

In the digital age, remixing is a prevalent form of play. In *The Pirate's Dilemma,* Mason says, "remixing is about taking something that already exists and redefining it in your own personal creative space, reinterpreting someone else's work your way." Put another way, Stephen B. Sample says, "Most new inventions are merely novel combinations of devices or techniques that already exist. Thus, the key to successful invention often lies in getting one's brain to imagine new combinations of existing elements that solve a problem in a way no one has ever thought of before." Creativity may or may not be original. Remember in the digital age the worth of an innovation is determined by the consumer. On the UGRR, the value of an innovation was measured in blood.

Remixing is what the open source movement on the Internet allows computer programmers to do. They can see what someone else is working on and create their own versions, building upon previous work. This is similar to what would happen on the Underground Railroad; enslaved Africans and conductors would adapt other escape plans and tweak them for their own use. Whether changing songs, codes, or direction, remixing can be beneficial.

Using Mason's Quick Mix Theory, here is an example of how to remix something. He suggests the following ingredients: you need to have a big idea; know who your audience, consumers, or users are; have information about who has already done what you're trying to do; and have a "pinch of originality." This is exactly what Mason did in his book, remixing game theory to support his premise. "Game theory examines situations where multiple players in a game make decisions based on what the other players will do, like an academic version of poker." Mason goes on to explain the "Prisoner's Dilemma", a game developed by the RAND Corporation in the 1950s.

In the game, two prisoners have been arrested for burglary. The police don't know if either, neither, or only one of them has participated in the crime. The dilemma is that if both prisoners confess, they'll receive a two-year sentence. If neither one will confess, they'll both receive a lighter sentence for possession of stolen goods. If one confesses and the other does not, one person will walk while the other will serve the maximum sentence of five years. The assumption is people will most likely act in self-interest. "Both prisoners would get lower sentences if they cooperated with each other and remained silent, but assuming the other will most likely snitch out of self-interest, their best choice is always to do the same."

Part of Mason's remix is using the Prisoner's Dilemma to explain the Pirate's Dilemma. "In the Pirate's Dilemma, Players A and B are not burglars but individuals or companies selling competing products. The players are not threatened by police, but by pirates: those creating a new space outside of the traditional, legitimate market." When pirates add value to society, society will support them, presenting a dilemma for established companies. If they fight the pirates, they may run afoul of public sensibilities, à la the recording industry. Mason asserts that if both companies fight piracy, they will only make money in the existing market, but lose money to pirates and add minimum value to society. If one company decides to fight piracy while the other competes, society will gain moderate value, and the company fighting piracy will lose while the one competing with the pirates will gain. Finally, if both companies decide to compete with the pirates (for example, creating new services like iTunes), both will gain profits in the emerging market and society will benefit as well. From this excerpt in his biography, Apple pioneer Steve Jobs agrees with Mason. "He (Steve) knew, however, that the best way to stop piracy—in fact the only way—was to offer an alternative that was more attractive than the brain-dead services that music companies were concocting." Jobs understood why music was being pirated beyond the obvious reason because it could be: "There was no alternative."

Before the Prisoner's and Pirate's Dilemmas, enslaved Africans faced a dilemma of their own. If they were in a group, they had to decide whether to remain together or to separate. If one was caught, all had to wonder if they would reveal the location of the others; after all, this is how several slave revolts were made known. In slavery, whether the slave talked or remained silent, he or she could be savagely beaten or killed. Linking gaming and the Underground Railroad may seem like an awkward connection, yet it has to be noted that innovation may involve elements of play. Even on the UGRR, the dynamics of play, in the form of gaming, strategy, risk, and even fragments of fun, were present.

SUMMARY

- Play involves game dynamics, strategy, humor and more.
- The majority of workers have always been used to make a minority wealthy.
- There are four defining characteristics of games: a goal, rules, a feedback loop, and voluntary participation.
- Examples of four game dynamics are: the appointment dynamic, status and influence, progression, and communal discovery.
- An epic win represents a huge come-from-behind victory through a team effort using unorthodox strategy.
- Augmented, virtual, and alternate reality allow consumers to access information in real time, to immerse themselves in an experience, and to incorporate elements of real life and gaming, respectively.
- Remixing is a form of play.
- The Prisoner's Dilemma, the Pirate's Dilemma, and the Innovator's Dilemma all depend on individual choice. The prisoners, the pirates, and the executives must determine the best move.

CHAPTER TWELVE

Rewinding the Future

"...to understand the future, you have to look back

at least twice as far as you're looking ahead."

JANE MCGONIGAL

The Underground Railroad is among the most effective, disruptive, and innovative networks in American history. Its origins are unclear, yet its impact cannot be ignored. People often ask why is something relevant and why should they care. It's a reasonable question. The UGRR is incredibly relevant, not only because of its historical impact on freedom in America, but also for the lessons learned from the network can be applied today. It provides a wealth of information for many pressing modern-day issues, including leadership, systems, access, freedom, movements, boundaries, innovation, and more.

Whether discussing the UGRR or the Internet, the architects for each system are innovators, individuals with the ability to solve problems, stand on principles, identify the purpose, shift their perspective, embrace their passion, pioneer a new path, and play their way to success, creating new ways to make things happen.

Abolitionists, the enslaved, and free men and women used their collective intuitions, insights, and imaginations to change the course of history. The enslaved did what they were told could not be done: they helped bring down the institution of slavery. Americans are known for their ingenuity, but slave narratives are often left out of the discussions involving innovation. It is a gross and detrimental oversight.

Enslaved Africans should be counted among the most innovative people in the history of America. They solved problems while literally in chains, but their struggles were not just physical; they had to overcome extreme psychological abuse as well. If just one enslaved individual could control their mind to secure freedom under harshly unforgiving circumstances, why is it so difficult for some to recognize and embrace the innovative mindset shift needed today? The enslaved must be recognized for innovating under fire. Some made excuses while others made it happen. This behavior is evident in modern society. The definition of insanity is repeating the same actions and expecting different results, yet many people do exactly that. This thinking is detrimental, and is hindering professionals, students, and private citizens alike.

This book connects the past with the present to provide better insight for the future. What doesn't work is clear: controlled, closed systems and minds are a hindrance. Understanding the role the UGRR played in history is vitally important; without this knowledge, facts can easily be changed. For example, in 2010 the Texas Board of Education's vote to change the word slavery to "the Atlantic triangular trade" in textbooks. During the same session, they moved to change the word "capitalism" to "free enterprise" and to minimize Thomas Jefferson's discussion regarding the separation of church and state.

The funny part is now the whole world can contribute to and research the truth; to alter it domestically means not only misrepresenting the information for American citizens, but global ones as well. People need the truth to be knowledgeable, and as long as freedom, access, and boundaries remain paramount issues, there will be a need for movements, organizations, and other interventions. Consumers now define quality, and gatekeepers of knowledge no longer have sole control. Continuing with the UGRR and modern workplace analogy, "enslaved" workers have more decision-making power while too many managers fight to maintain the status quo. Remember that during slavery only a minority of White males in the South owned enslaved Africans, yet they wanted political power disproportionate to their numbers; isn't it funny how history seemingly repeats? Understanding what happened in the past provides invaluable insight in the present.

Revisiting the seven elements of innovation in light of the digital age, the Underground Railroad was a leaderless movement formed to address a specific problem. Harriet Tubman realized early on she couldn't tell everyone everything or certain people anything, and was such an effective innovator that a bounty was placed on her head. In some corporations, the out-of-the-box thinkers are branded as troublemakers as well. As a conductor, Tubman had multiple routes to safety. She improvised and then added options she could not consider because she didn't know what they were in advance. She engaged in just-in-time learning on a daily basis. These are qualities leaders must possess today. Flexibility and adaptability are necessary skills.

As Dr. Clayton Christensen, the father of the study of disruption, suggests, it's most effective to provide independent thinkers with freedom and resources to experiment. Conformity kills originality, creativity, and innovation, and is a dangerous status to maintain. Some of the enslaved refused to conform. Their rejection of unfair practices led them to create unimagined solutions to pressing problems, whereas some enslaved Africans, like some workers today, could not think independently. This is learned behavior. Innovators create convenient solutions that save people time and money. On the Underground Railroad, innovators saved even more: people's lives.

The most successful innovators are typically propelled by circumstances beyond their control. They are not only forced to create a solution, but must implement it as well. They are so internally driven that they are compelled by their passion to innovate. In *Drive*, Daniel Pink would call this Motivation 3.0, which focuses on mastery, autonomy, and purpose. No matter the catalyst, change and progress must be made.

The enslaved and their supporters did what had to be done to change the course of history. They used tools, intellect, and courage to alter their fates, freeing themselves and future generations. Fundamentally, innovation is all about perspective. The enslaved changed their perspectives and perceptions in order to exist on and off of the plantation. Educator, philosopher, and activist Dr. W.E.B. Dubois would describe this as duality and/or duplicity. The enslaved acted one way in public and another way at home. This passage from Dubois' book, *The Souls of Black Folk*, is often used to describe the experience of some Blacks in America:

> "It is a peculiar sensation, this double-consciousness, this sense of always looking at one's self through the eyes of others, of measuring one's soul by the tape of a world that looks on in amused contempt and pity. One ever feels his twoness,—an American, a Negro; two warring souls, two thoughts, two unreconciled strivings; two warring ideals in one dark body, whose dogged strength alone keeps it from being torn asunder." The slaves were so innovative they assumed dual personalities in order to make it to freedom. Their mindset was malleable."

This passage has been shared deliberately to make more people aware of the powerful duality inherent in the lives of both the enslaved and their descendants.

Let's be clear: the UGRR was not a game, yet the strategies employed utilized game dynamics. Play is an important element to consider when examining innovation, and younger companies include play as a professional tenet; their workers are more productive and creative as a result. Some conductors treated their roles in a playful manner to offset the fear they experienced. The UGRR is an example of an epic win, the ultimate prize in the world of gaming.

History will not be kind to those in power in the twenty-first century who refuse to embrace change. With more access than ever before to resources, wisdom, and other amenities, if those in control continue to refuse to change, just like the slaves who remained on the plantation out of fear even after the Civil War and the passing of the 13th Amendment, it will be a sad time for America. If the past trumps the present and rules the future in the digital age, America will lose again and the number of casualties will be even more devastating.

The purpose of this book is to argue that the Underground Railroad is among the most disruptive, effective, and innovative networks in the United States' history. In addition, I have provided a framework for innovation, utilizing examples from the Underground Railroad. The enslaved could not succeed within the given system: if they sat still, they would have died in bondage, but if they fought, they may have been killed for their actions. Out-of-the-box thinking was the only thing that could improve their situation. The need for innovation is just as pressing in twenty-first century America.

The Internet was initially created for research to serve the Department of Defense and the academic community, but from those humble beginnings has grown exponentially, connecting people around the world to a degree never before thought possible. A labyrinth that allows people to transcend the confines of their physical workspace, the Internet, like the Underground Railroad, facilitates unprecedented opportunities for freedom, even if this venue for creation is sometimes in direct conflict with people who feel they have a "right" to control people.

When did the most effective, innovative, and disruptive network in U.S. history dissolve? It didn't. According to Fergus Bordewich, author of *Bound for Canaan*, "There was, of course, no official termination to the Underground Railroad." It exists in the hearts and minds of those who are still fighting for freedom. In *Make Free*, author William Breyfogle said, "Finally, when its work was done and the time allotted it had run out, it disappeared from sight, leaving scarcely a rack behind."

It is this author's hope that this discussion of slavery, viewed through a different lens using the Seven Elements of Innovation, will provide a concrete blueprint for the future discussions about innovation, evaluation, and assessment. More importantly, the legacy of enslaved Africans will encourage and empower you to continue the fight for justice and freedom. When access and freedom are controlled or compromised, people innovate. That's what some of the enslaved and those working on the Underground Railroad did. The legendary abolitionist, activist, and orator Frederick Douglass famously said, "Agitate! Agitate! Agitate!" In the twenty-first century, Dr. Syb says "Innovate! Innovate! Innovate!"

SUMMARY

- The Underground Railroad is among the most effective, disruptive, and innovative networks in American history.

- To ignore the role and relevance of the UGRR, the enslaved Africans, abolitionists, conductors, and anti-slavery supporters does a grave disservice to present and future generations.

- It is an Orwellian moment as the Texas Board of Education votes to change historical language, affecting content and context.

- Dr. Syb's Seven Elements of Innovation (problem, principle, purpose, perspective, pioneering, passion and play) are not mutually inclusive or exclusive. They can be used individually, collectively, or in part to examine, assess, and evaluate anything from work performance to classroom success and more.

- The UGRR never ceased operation.

- Conformity kills, while creativity empowers. It's the equivalent of handing someone a fish versus teaching them how to fish.

REFERENCES

BOOKS

Anderson, Chris. *Free: How Today's Smartest Businesses Profit by Giving Something for Nothing*. New York: Hyperion, 2010.

Anderson, Chris. *The Long Tail: Why the Future of Business is Selling Less of More*. New York: Hyperion, 2006.

Benkler, Yochai. *The Wealth of Networks: How Social Production Transforms Markets and Freedom*. New Haven: Yale University Press. 2006.

Bennett, Sybril. *The Role of Race in Black Student Intragroup Peer Interactions: A Qualitative Analysis*. Ph.D. diss., Vanderbilt University, 1999.

Bradford, Sarah. *Harriet Tubman: The Moses of Her People*. Mineola: Dover Publications, Inc., 2004.

Breyfogle, William. *Make Free: The Story of the Underground Railroad*. Philadelphia: J.B. Lippincott Company, 1958.

Bolman, Lee. & Terrence Deal. *Reframing Organizations: Artistry, Choice, and Leadership*. San Francisco: Jossey-Bass 2003.

Bordewich, Fergus. *Bound for Canaan: The Epic Story of the Underground Railroad, America's First Civil Rights Movement*. New York: Harper Paperbacks, 2005.

Buckmaster, Henrietta. *Let My People Go: The Story of the Underground Railroad and the Growth of the Abolition Movement*. Charleston: University of South Carolina Press, 1992.

Christensen, Clayton, M., Curtis W. Johnson and Michael B. Horn. *Disrupting Class: How Disruptive Innovation Will Change the Way the World Learns*. New York: McGraw-Hill Professional, 2008.

Christensen, Clayton, M. *The Innovator's Dilemma: The Revolutionary Book That Will Change the Way You Do Business*. Boston: Harvard Business School Press, 1997.

Christensen, Clayton. *The Innovative University: Changing the DNA of Higher Education from the Inside Out*. San Francisco: Jossey-Bass, 2011.

Collins, J. *Good to Great: Why Some Companies Make the Leap...and Others Don't*. New York: Harper Business, 2001.

127

Danforth, Mildred, E. *A Quaker Pioneer: Laura Haviland, Superintendent of the Underground Railroad.* New York: Exposition Press, 1961.

Davis, F. James. *Who Is Black?: One Nation's Definition.* Philadelphia: Pennsylvania State University Press, 2001.

Dawkins, Marcia Alesan. *Clearly Invisible: Racial Passing and the Color of Cultural Identity.* Waco: Baylor University Press, 2012.

Dewar, James. A. "The Information Age and the Printing Press: Looking Backward to See Ahead." http://www.rand.org/pubs/papers/P8014.html. Santa Monica: Rand Corporation, 2011.

Dubois, W. E. Burghardt. *The Souls of Black Folk.* Chicago: A.C. McClurg & Co., 1903.

Foote, Neil. *Haternation: How Incivility and Racism are Dividing Us.* (Los Gatos, CA: Smashwords, 2012), Multiple format e-book, http://www.smashwords.com/books/view/247429.

Franklin, J. H. (1967). *From Slavery To Freedom, Third Edition : A History of Negro Americans,* 3rd ed. New York: Alfred A. Knopf, Inc, 1971.

Friedman, Thomas, L. *The World is Flat: A Brief History of the Twenty-first Century.* New York: Farrar Straus & Giroux, 2005.

Gara, Larry. *The Liberty Line: The Legend of the Underground Railroad.* Lexington: University of Kentucky Press, 1961.

Gladwell, Malcolm. *Blink: The Power of Thinking Without Thinking.* New York: Back Bay Books, 2007.

Gladwell, Malcolm. *Outliers: The Story of Success.* New York: Back Bay Books, 2011

Gladwell, Malcolm. *The Tipping Point: How Little Things Can Make a Big Difference.* New York: Back Bay Books, 2002.

Godin, Seth. *Tribes: We Need You to Lead Us.* New York, NY: Portfolio Trade, 2008.

Godin, Seth. *Linchpin: Are you indispensable?* New York: Portfolio Trade, 2011.

Gonzalez, Jose and Juan Torres. *News for All People: The Epic Story of Race and the American Media.* New York: Verso Books, 2011.

Hagedorn, Ann. *Beyond the River: The Untold Story of the Heroes of the Underground Railroad.* New York: Simon & Schuster, 2004.

Harrold, Stanley. *Border War: Fighting Over Slavery Before the Civil War.* Chapel Hill: The University of North Carolina Press, 2010.

Harvey, Steve. *Act Like a Lady, Think Like a Man: What Men Really Think About Love, Relationships, Intimacy, and Commitment.* New York: Amistad, 2011.

Hodges, Graham Russell Gao. *David Ruggles: A Radical Black Abolitionist and the Underground Railroad in New York City.* Chapel Hill: The University of North Carolina Press, 2010.

Huxley, Aldous. *Brave New World.* New York: Harper Perennial Modern Classics, 2006.

Isaacson, Walter. *Steve Jobs.* New York: Simon and Schuster, 2011.

Jacobs, Hariett. *Incidents in the Life of a Slave Girl.* New York: Simon and Brown, 2012.

Jarvis, Jeff. *What Would Google Do? Reverse-Engineering the Fastest Growing Company in the History of the World.* New York:Harper Business, 2011.

Johnson, Spencer. *Who Moved My Cheese?* New York: G.P. Putnam's Sons, 1998.

Kane, Pat. "*The Play Ethic: A Manifesto for a Different Way of Living*" (September, 2005) quoted in Daniel Pink, *A Whole New Mind: Why Right-Brainers Will Rule the Future* (New York, NY: Riverhead Trade, 2006)

Kent, Peter. *Search Engine Optimization for Dummies.* Hoboken: For Dummies, 2012.

Loewen, James. *Lies My Teacher Told Me Everything your American History Textbook Got Wrong.* New York: Touchstone, 2007.

Mason, Matt. *The Pirate's Dilemma: How Youth Culture is Reinventing Capitalism.* New York, NY: Free Press, 2009.

McGonigal, Jane. *Reality is Broken: Why Games Make Us Better and How They Can Change the World.* New York: Penguin Books, 2011.

Moore, Marc, A. *The Art of War.* Raleigh: Sweetwater Press, 2004.

Olsen, Christopher. J. *The American Civil War: A Hands-on History.* New York, NY: Hill and Wang, 2007.

Orwell, George. *1984.* New York: Signet Classic, 1950.

Parker, John and Stuart Seeley Sprague. *His Promised Land: The Autobiography of John P. Parker Former Slave and Conductor on the Underground Railroad.* New York: W. W. Norton & Company, 1996.

Pink, Daniel. *Drive: The Surprising Truth about What Motivates Us.* New York, NY: Riverhead Books, 2009.

Pink, Daniel. *A Whole New Mind: Why Right-Brainers Will Rule the Future.* New York, NY: Riverhead Trade, 2006.

Postman, Neil. *Amusing Ourselves to Death: Public Discourse in the Age of Show Business.* New York: Penguin Books, 2005.

Poynter, Dan. *Dan Poynter's Self-Publishing Manual: How to Write, Print and Sell Your Own Book.* Santa Barbara, CA: Para Publishing, 2007.

Qualman, Erik. *Digital Leader: 5 Simple Keys to Success and Influence.* New York: McGraw-Hill, 2011.

Qualman, Erik. *Socialnomics: How Social Media Transforms the Way We Live and Do Business.* Hoboken: Wiley, 2010.

Richmond, Ben. *Reminiscences of Levi Coffin.* Richmond, IN: Friends United Press, 2001.

Rifkin, Jeremy. *The Age of Access: The New Culture of Hypercapitalism Where All of Life is a Paid-for Experience.* New York: Tarcher, 2001.

Robinson, Sir Ken. *Out of Our Minds: Learning to be Creative.* North Mankato, MN: Capstone, 2001.

Rogers, Everett. *Diffusion of Innovations*, 5th, Edition. New York: Free Press, 2003.

Russell-Cole, Kathy, Midge Wilson and Ronald Hall. *The Color Complex: The Politics of Skin Color in a New Millennium.* New York, Anchor, 2013.

Sample, Stephen B. *The Contrarian's Guide to Leadership.* San Francisco: Jossey-Bass, 2003.

Shirky, Clay. *Here Comes Everybody: The Power of Organizing Without Organizations.* New York: Penguin Books, 2009.

Siebert, Wilbur H. *The Underground Railroad from Slavery to Freedom: A Comprehensive History.* Mineola, MN: Dover Publications, 2006.

Still, William. *The Underground Railroad: Authentic Narratives and First-hand Accounts.* Mineola, MN: Dover Publications, 2007.

Stowe, Harriet Beecher. *Uncle Tom's Cabin.* Mineola: Dover Publications, 2005.

Surowiecki, James. *The Wisdom of Crowds.* New York, NY.: Anchor-Knopf Publishing House, 2005.

Taylor, William and Polly LaBarre. *Mavericks at Work: Why the Most Original Minds in Business Win.* New York, NY: Harper Paperbacks, 2007.

Warren, Rick. *The Purpose-Driven Life: What on Earth am I Here For?* Grand Rapids: Zondervan, 2002.

NON-BOOK REFERENCES

Databases

Wilbur H. Siebert Collection Microfilm Edition, MIC 192, the Ohio Historical Society Archives/
   Library.
Dr. Isaac Beck to Wilbur Siebert regarding Underground Railroad, December 14, 1892 from Wilbur
   H. Siebert Collection.
Capt. R.C. Rankin to Wilbur Siebert regarding Underground Railroad, April 8, 1892 from Wilbur H.
   Siebert Collection.
Alexander Ross to Wilbur Siebert regarding Underground Railroad, August 2, 1896 from Wilbur H.
   Siebert Collection.

Movies

Ethnic Notions, directed by Marlon Riggs (California Newsreel, 1986).
Lincoln, directed by Steven Spielberg (Dreamworks Pictures/Twentieth Century Fox, 2012).
Miss Representation directed by Jennifer Siebel Newsom (Girls Club Entertainment, 2011).

Newspapers and Periodicals

Henry Bibb, *Voice of the Fugitive,* February 26, 1852.
John Johnston, "The Underground Railroad," *The Cincinnati Enquirer,* June 19, 1994.
William Lloyd Garrison, "To the Public" *The Liberator,* January 1, 1831, sec. 1, p. 1.
Lynn Norment, "Prince Reclaims His Throne," *Ebony Magazine,* September, 2004: 196-202.
John Rankin, "Life of Rev. John Rankin," from the collection of Lobena and Charles Frost, 1872.
"Men Who Worked on the Underground Railroad," *The Commercial Tribune,* February 18, 1900.
"Anti-Slavery Meeting", *The Ripley Bee,* January 10, 1852.
The Ripley Bee, February 16, 1856.
Article on Henry Bibb. *The Ripley Bee,* April 9, 1853

Peer Reviews

Marcia Alesan Dawkins, Clinical Assistant Professor of Communications, University of Southern Cal-
   ifornia, Annenberg, Los Angeles, CA.
Nathan Griffith, Associate Professor of Political Science, Belmont University, Nashville, TN.
Shelley W. Jeffcoat, Author, *When Fathers Were Gods and Children Ruled.*
Peter Kuryla, Assistant Professor of History, Belmont University, Nashville, TN.
Matt Mason, Author, *The Pirate's Dilemma.*
Kim Pearson, Associate Professor of English, The College of New Jersey, Ewing, NJ.
Erik Qualman, Author, *Digital Leader: 5 Simple Keys to Success and Influence* and *Socialnomics: How Social
   Media Transforms the Way We Live and Do Business.*
Monique Wilson, Doctoral of Management in Community College Policy and Administration Can-
   didate, University Maryland, University College, Adelphi, Maryland.

Site Visits

Abbotsford Historic Home of Sir Walter Scott "*The Lady of the Lake.*" Melrose, Scotland, summer, 2006.

Battlefield at Gettysburg, Gettysburg National Military Park, Adams County, Pennsylvania, summer, 2007.

Boston African American National Historic Site, Boston, Massachusetts, summer, 2007.

Frederick Douglass House National Historic Site, Washington, D.C., summer, 2004.

Historic Home of Abolitionist and Foundry Owner, John Parker, Ripley, Ohio, summer, 2011.

The National Underground Freedom Center, Cincinnati, Ohio, summer, 2007.

Union Township Public Library, Ripley, Ohio, summer, 2010.

The Rankin House, National Historic Landmark and Underground Railroad Station, Ripley, Ohio, summer, 2010.

Unpublished Interviews

Carl Westmoreland, interview by author, Cincinnati, Ohio, summer, 2010.

Alison Gibson, interview by author, Ripley, Ohio, summer, 2010.

Websites

Clayton Christensen, http://www.claytonchristensen.com/, accessed summer, 2012.

National Underground Railroad Freedom Center, "Company Overview," http://www.freedom-center.org/, accessed summer, 2008.

National Archives and Records Administration, http://www.archives.gov/exhibits/featured_documents/emancipation_proclamation/transcript.html accessed fall, 2012.

National Park Service, http://www.nps.gov/liho/historyculture/debates.htm, accessed fall, 2012. Public Broadcasting Service (PBS), "The Compromise of 1850 and the Fugitive Slave Act," http://www.pbs.org/wgbh/aia/part4/4p2951.html, accessed fall, 2012.

Author's Notes

Wikipedia was used as a general source throughout this project. Information was triangulated with other sources. Sources were documented based on the Harvard Business School Citation Guide, 2012-13 Academic Year.

"Even when you whisper, your voice carries." That's basically what the nuns used to tell me. Then, I don't think it was a compliment. Now, it's a responsibility taken very seriously. With degrees from Vanderbilt University, Loyola University of Chicago, and Marquette University, the value of my voice has increased dramatically. As a navy brat and a product of Catholic schools, discipline and education were (and still are!) synonymous. Mind you, I never focused on being an author or a professor. My goal was to become a news anchor.

For nearly twenty years, I worked behind the scenes in television newsrooms in Milwaukee and Chicago and on camera in Nashville. The experience built my character, my conscience, and my comedic repertoire. Oh, to work in television news, one must maintain a sense of humor. A chance encounter with a future mentor guided my path to Belmont University in Nashville, Tennessee. I've been teaching on and off since 1995 and consistently since 2003. It was a timely transition as the analog world abruptly switched to a digital one. Being forced to learn as much as possible about social and digital media tools catapulted me into the virtual world. Fate has a funny way of preparing you for your destiny and making sure you arrive on time.

Some people describe me using the following words: passionate, intelligent, troublemaker, serious, ambitious, responsible, and honest. During a women's retreat, they asked us to create an acronym to describe ourselves. Mine was STAR: speaker, teacher, actress, and reporter. No matter the platform, my mission in life is clear: to educate, engage, and empower people, giving them access to information, resources, and networks.

As an educator, speaker, consultant, journalist, facilitator, actress, and advisor, my voice still carries. Want to hear what else I have to say? Follow me on Twitter (@drsyb), or get on my speaking calendar (drsyb7@gmail.com). Or, if you're just plain nosy like me, Google me.

—Sybril "Dr. Syb" Bennett, Ph.D.

Sybril Bennett, Ph.D., affectionately known as "Dr. Syb", is an associate professor of journalism at Belmont University in Nashville, Tennessee. Dr. Syb is a two-time Emmy Award winning journalist. She also authored The Color-Full Alphabet Book. Follow Dr. Syb on Twitter (@drsyb or @innovateugrr), and visit innovateugrr.com or drsyb.com for more information.  See her TEDxNashville 2013 presentation on YouTube or hear her podcast at etpcast.com. Feel free to contact her at innovateugrr@gmail.com.

AUTHOR PHOTO:

Daniel DuVerney Photography, www.duverneyphoto.com

Makeup by Marcus Geeter, www.marcusgeetermakeupartist.com

JACKET DESIGN:

Ventress Design Works, www.ventress.com

Spike photograph by Tom Ventress

CPSIA information can be obtained at www.ICGtesting.com
Printed in the USA
LVOW08s1947060214

372463LV00004B/3/P